MW00745527

Latin American Spanish phrasebook

Talia Bugel

with
Gloria Arizaga
Alicia Burga
Mercedes Paz

New York   Chicago   San Francisco   Lisbon   London   Madrid   Mexico City
Milan   New Delhi   San Juan   Seoul   Singapore   Sydney   Toronto

ISBN-10: 0-07-148628-3
ISBN-13: 978-0-07-148628-6

McGraw-Hill books are available at special quantity discounts to use as
premiums and sales promotions, or for use in corporate training programs.
For more information, please write to the Director of Special Sales,
Professional Publishing, McGraw-Hill, Two Penn Plaza, New York, NY
10121-2298. Or contact your local bookstore

Editor & Project Manager
Kate Nicholson

Prepress
Nicolas Echallier

The publishers wish to thank Andrew Hastings and Fernando Léon Solis for
their work on *Chambers Spanish Phrasebook*, which served as the base text
for this book, as well as Carol Braham for her advice on American English.

CONTENTS

CONTENTS

INTRODUCTION

This brand new English-Latin American Spanish phrasebook from Harrap is ideal for anyone wishing to try out their foreign language skills while travelling abroad. The information is practical and clearly presented, helping you to overcome the language barrier and mix with the locals.

Each section features a list of useful words and a selection of common phrases: some of these you will read or hear, while others will help you to express yourself. The simple phonetic transcription system, specifically designed for English speakers, ensures that you will always make yourself understood.

The book also includes a mini bilingual dictionary of around 5,000 words, so that more adventurous users can build on the basic structures and engage in more complex conversations.

Concise information on local culture and customs is provided, along with practical tips to save you time. After all, you're on holiday – time to relax and enjoy yourself! There is also a food and drink glossary to help you make sense of menus, and ensure that you don't miss out on any of the national or regional specialities.

Remember that any effort you make will be appreciated. So don't be shy – have a go!

ABBREVIATIONS USED IN THIS GUIDE

Am	American English	*adj*	adjective
Arg	Argentina	*adv*	adverb
Br	British English	*f*	feminine noun
Carib	Caribbean	*fpl*	feminine plural noun
Mex	Mexico	*m*	masculine noun
		mpl	masculine plural noun
		n	noun
		pl	plural
		prep	preposition
		sing	singular
		v	verb

PRONUNCIATION

In Spanish, words are pronounced as they are written, so once you master a few simple rules you will be able to read it correctly. Although Spanish speakers from both sides of the Atlantic can easily understand each other, they pronounce some sounds differently. In this book we give the most common Latin American pronunciation.

Vowels

a	like the *a* in *father*, but slightly shorter
e	like the *e* in *men*, but slightly longer
i	like *ee* in *seen*, but slightly shorter
o	like the *o* in *hot*, but slightly longer
u	like *oo* in *spoon*, but slightly shorter

Consonants

b, **v**	these are pronounced in exactly the same way. In an initial position, and after **m**, like *b* in *butter*; elsewhere, the lips vibrate, but do not actually close to stop the flow of air.
c	before **a**, **o** and **u**, like *ck* in *back*; before **e** and **i**, like *s* in *sit*
d	like *d* in *dead*
g	before **a**, **o** and **u**, like *g* in *gag*; before **e** and **i**, like *ch* in Scottish *loch* or German *Bach*

Note that in the combinations **gue** and **gui**, the **u** is silent unless written with a diaeresis (**ü**).

h	always silent
j	like *ch* in Scottish *loch* or German *Bach*
ll	similar to *y* in *yet*
ñ	like *ny* in *canyon*
qu	like *ck* in *back*
r	a lightly rolled *r*: tap your tongue once on the ridge behind your top teeth
rr	a strongly rolled *r*, Scottish-style
v	see **b**, above

| **w** | only found in loan words, pronounced as in English |
| **z** | like s in *sit* |

Other consonants (f, k, l, m, n, p, s) are pronounced as in English.

For every sentence written in Spanish in this guide, you will find the pronunciation given in italics. If you follow this phonetic transcription, you will be able to make yourself understood in Spanish. Do bear in mind, though, that this is a simplified system intended to help you produce reasonably understandable Spanish. Some Spanish sounds don't exist in English, and so we have used the codes below to transcribe them.

Remember to stress the syllables in **bold**.

ah	as in *car, father*
air	as in *fair, wear*
aw	as in *cause, paws*
ay	as in *day, sleigh*
ee	as in *tree, flea, field*
eye	as in *I, my, eye*
oh	as in *go, throw, although*
oo	as in *soon, spoon*
ow	as in *cow, how, now*
ch	as in *cheese, church*
CH	as in Scottish *loch* or German *Bach*
RR	a strongly rolled r, Scottish-style

Alphabet

a	*ah*	**k**	*kah*	**t**	*tay*
b	*bay*	**l**	*el-ay*	**u**	*oo*
c	*say*	**m**	*em-ay*	**v**	*bay*
d	*day*	**n**	*en-ay*	**w**	*bay doh-blay/*
e	*ay*	**ñ**	*en-yay*		*doh-blay bay*
f	*ef-ay*	**o**	*oh*	**x**	*ek-ees*
g	*CHay*	**p**	*pay*	**y**	*ee gree-ay-ga*
h	*a-chay*	**q**	*koo*	**z**	*say-ta*
i	*ee*	**r**	*eRR-ay*		
j	*CHoh-ta*	**s**	*es-ay*		

EVERYDAY CONVERSATION

People in Latin America generally kiss each other on the cheek when saying hello or goodbye. You can use the familiar "tú" form of address when speaking to people of your own age or younger, even if you don't know them very well. When speaking to older people or business associates, it is advisable to use the polite "usted" form until they suggest doing otherwise. Note that **usted** is conjugated like the third person (singular for **usted** and plural for **ustedes**); this is because the word is derived from the expression **Vuestra Merced**, meaning "Your Grace". The use of "usted" is more widespread in rural areas and villages than in cities.

Buenos días is used as a greeting from morning until lunchtime. **Buenas tardes** is used in the afternoon until it gets dark, and **buenas noches** at night. Although there are no hard and fast rules, you are likely to hear **buenas noches** from about 10 p.m. in summer and as early as 6 p.m. in winter.

The basics

bye	adiós *ad-yohs*, (Peru, Arg) chau *chow*
excuse me	(interrupting) perdone *pair-doh-nay*; (getting past someone) permiso *pair-mee-soh*
good afternoon	buenas tardes *bway-nas tar-days*
good evening	buenas tardes *bway-nas tar-days*
good morning	buenos días *bway-nos dee-as*
good night	buenas noches *bway-nas no-chays*
hello, hi	hola *oh-la*
no	no *noh*
OK	de acuerdo *day a-kwair-doh*, (Mex, Peru) okey *o-kay*, (Arg) bueno *bway-noh*
please	por favor *por fa-bor*
see you later	hasta luego *as-ta lway-goh*
see you soon	hasta pronto *as-ta pron-toh*

see you tomorrow	hasta mañana *as-ta man-yah-na*
thank you	gracias *gras-yas*
yes	sí *see*

Expressing yourself

I'd like...
quisiera...
kees-yair-a...

we'd like...
quisiéramos...
kees-yair-a-mos...

do you want...?
¿quiere...?
kyair-ay...

do you have...?
¿tiene...?
tyen-ay...

is there a...?
¿hay un...?
eye oon...

are there any...?
¿hay...?
eye...

where is...?
¿dónde está...?
don-day es-ta...

where are...?
¿dónde están...?
don-day es-tan...

how...?
¿cómo...?
koh-moh...

why...?
¿por qué...?
por-kay...

when...?
¿cuándo...?
kwan-doh...

what...?
¿qué...?
kay...

how much is it?
¿cuánto es?
kwan-toh es

what is it?
¿qué es?
kay es

do you speak English?
¿habla usted inglés?
ab-la oos-ted eeng-glays

where are the *(Am)* restrooms *or (Br)* toilets, please?
¿por favor, dónde están los baños?
por fa-bor, don-day es-tan los ban-yohs

how are you?
¿cómo está?
koh-moh es-ta

fine, how are you?
bien, ¿y tú?
byen, ee too

fine, thanks
muy bien, gracias
mwee byen, gras-yas

I'm sorry
perdón, *(Mex)* lo siento, *(Peru)* disculpe
pair-don/loh syen-toh/dees-cool-pay

yes please
sí, por favor
see, por fa-bor

no thanks
no, gracias
noh, gras-yas

thanks a lot
muchas gracias
moo-chas gras-yas

you're welcome
de nada
day nah-da

Understanding

abierto	open
averiado	out of order
baños	*(Am)* restrooms, *(Br)* toilets
cerrado	closed
cuidado	attention
entrada	entrance
entrada libre	free entry
malogrado *(Peru)*	out of order
prohibido…	no…, do not…
reservado	reserved
roto	out of order
salida	exit

hay…
there is/are…

bienvenido/bienvenida
welcome

¿le importa que…?
do you mind if…?

un momento, por favor
one moment please

siéntese, por favor
please sit down

PROBLEMS UNDERSTANDING SPANISH

Expressing yourself

pardon?
¿cómo?
koh-moh

what?
¿qué?
kay

could you repeat that?
¿lo puede repetir?
loh pway-day re-pe-tir

could you speak more slowly, please?
¿podría hablar más despacio, por favor?
pod-ree-a ab-lar mas des-pas-yoh, por fa-bor?

I don't understand
no entiendo
noh en-tyen-doh

I didn't understand
no he entendido
noh ay en-ten-dee-doh

I understand a little bit
entiendo un poquito
en-tyen-doh oon poh-kee-toh

I don't understand a thing
no entiendo nada
noh en-tyen-doh nah-da

I can understand a bit of Spanish but I can't speak it
entiendo un poco de español, pero no sé hablarlo
en-tyen-doh oon poh-koh day es-pan-yol, pe-ro noh say ab-lar-lo

I can hardly speak any Spanish
hablo muy poco español
ab-loh mwee poh-koh es-pan-yol

I have difficulty understanding/speaking
me cuesta entender/hablar
may kwes-ta en-ten-dair/ab-lar

do you speak English?
¿habla inglés?
ab-la eeng-glays

how do you say... in Spanish?
¿cómo se dice... en español?
koh-moh say dee-say... en es-pan-yol

how do you spell it?
¿cómo se escribe?
*koh-moh say es-**kree**-bay*

what's that called?
¿cómo se llama eco?
*koh-moh say **yah**-ma **es**-oh*

could you write it down for me?
¿podría escribírmelo?
*pod-**ree**-a es-kree-**beer**-may-loh*

Understanding

¿entiende español?
do you understand Spanish?

significa...
it means...

se escribe...
it's spelled...

es un tipo de...
it's a type of...

TALKING ABOUT THE LANGUAGE

Expressing yourself

I learned a few words from a book
he aprendido algunas palabras con un libro
*ay ap-ren-**dee**-doh al-**goo**-nas pa-**la**-bras kon oon **lee**-broh*

I studied it at school but I've forgotten everything
lo estudié en la escuela pero se me ha olvidado todo
*loh es-tood-**yay** en la es-**kway**-la **pe**-ro say may a ol-bee-**dah**-doh **toh**-doh*

I can just about get by
me defiendo más o menos
*may def-**yen**-doh mas oh **may**-nos*

I hardly know two words!
no sé casi nada
*no say **ka**-see **nah**-da*

I find it difficult
me parece difícil
*may pa-**re**-say dee-**fee**-seel*

some of the sounds are hard to pronounce
hay sonidos difíciles de pronunciar
eye soh-nee-dohs dee-fee-see-les day proh-noon-syar

I know the basics but no more than that
tengo unas nociones pero nada más
teng-goh oo-nas noh-syoh-nays pe-ro nah-da mas

it's quite similar to French
se parece bastante al francés
say pa-re-say bas-tan-tay al fran-says

it helps to know a bit of Italian
saber un poco de italiano ayuda
sa-bair oon poh-koh day ee-tal-yah-noh eye-oo-da

people speak too quickly for me
la gente habla demasiado rápido
la CHen-tay ab-la day-mas-yah-doh ra-pee-doh

Understanding

hablas español muy bien
you speak very good Spanish

usted no tiene mucho acento
you don't have much of an accent

me parece que te defiendes muy bien
I think you manage very well (in Spanish)

ASKING THE WAY

Expressing yourself

excuse me, where is the...?
por favor, ¿dónde está…?
por fa-bor, don-day es-ta…

I'm looking for...
estoy buscando…
es-toy boos-kan-doh…

can you tell me how to get to...?
¿podría decirme cómo se va a...?
*pod-**ree**-a de-**seer**-may **koh**-moh say ba a...*

could you show me on the map?
¿me lo podría mostrar en el mapa?
*may loh pod-**ree**-a mos-**trar** en el **ma**-pa*

is there a map of the city/town somewhere?
¿hay un plano de la ciudad en algún sitio?
*eye oon **plah**-noh day la syoo-**dad** en al-**goon seet**-yoh*

is it far?
¿está lejos?
*es-ta **lay**-CHos*

I'm lost
me he perdido
*may ay pair-**dee**-doh*

I'm totally lost
estoy totalmente perdido/perdida
*es-**toy** toh-tal-**men**-tay pair-**dee**-do/pair-**dee**-da*

Understanding

bajar	to go down
continuar	to continue
dar media vuelta	to turn around
derecha	right
doblar	to turn
girar	to turn
izquierda	left
seguir	follow
subir	go up
todo defrente *(Peru)*, **todo derecho**, **todo recto**	straight ahead
torcer	to turn
voltear *(Peru)*	to turn

¿va caminando *or* **a pie?**
are you on foot?

está a cinco minutos en coche *or (Arg)* **en auto** *or (Mex, Peru)* **en carro**
it's five minutes away by car

es la primera/segunda/tercera calle a la derecha
it's the first/second/third street on the right

tome la primera calle a la izquierda después del semáforo
take the first street on the left after the traffic lights

tome la próxima salida
take the next exit

vaya/siga todo recto hasta un edificio grande y blanco
go/continue straight ahead until you get to a big white building

está muy cerca/bastante lejos/aquí al lado
it's very close/quite far away/right here

está ahí mismo/después del cruce
it's right there/just after the crossroads

ya lo verá, está señalizado
you'll see it, it's signposted

venga conmigo, lo acompaño
come with me, I'll take you

GETTING TO KNOW PEOPLE

The basics

bad	malo *mah-loh*
beautiful	(Arg) lindo *leen-doh*, (Mex, Peru) bonito *bo-nee-toh*, (Carib) chulo *choo-loh*
boring	aburrido *a-boo-RRee-doh*
cheap	barato *ba-rah-toh*
expensive	caro *kah-roh*
good	bueno *bway-noh*
great	estupendo *es-too-pen-doh*, excelente *ek-say-len-tay*, (Carib) chévere *chay-bell-ay*, (Arg, Mex) genial *CHen-yahl*
interesting	interesante *een-tay-ray-san-tay*
OK	(in agreement) está bien *es-ta byen*, (Mex, Peru) okey *oh-kay*, (Arg) bueno *bway-noh*; (not bad) bastante bien *bas-tan-tay byen*
well	bien *byen*
to hate	detestar *day-tes-tar*, odiar *oh-dyar*
to like	gustar *goos-tar*
to love	encantar *eng-kan-tar*

INTRODUCING YOURSELF AND FINDING OUT ABOUT OTHER PEOPLE

Expressing yourself

my name's...
me llamo...
may yah-moh...

what's your name?
¿cómo se llama?
koh-moh say yah-ma

let me introduce...
te/le presento a...
tay/lay pray-sen-toh a...

this is my husband
éste es mi marido
es-tay es mee ma-ree-doh

I'm American
soy estadounidense
soy es-tah-doh-oo-nee-den-say

I'm from...
soy de...
soy day...

how old are you?
¿cuántos años tiene?
kwan-tohs an-yohs tyen-ay

what do you do for a living?
¿a qué se dedica?
a kay say de-dee-ka

I work
trabajo
tra-ba-CHoh

I'm a teacher
soy profesor/profesora
soy pro-fes-or/pro-fes-aw-ra

I work part-time
trabajo a tiempo parcial
tra-ba-CHoh a tyem-poh par-syahl

I'm retired
estoy jubilado
es-toy CHoo-bee-lah-doh

I have two children
tengo dos hijos
teng-goh dos ee-CHohs

pleased to meet you!
¡encantado/a!
eng-kan-tah-doh/eng-kan-tah-da

this is my partner, Karen
ésta es mi compañera, Karen
es-ta es mee kom-pan-yair-a, ka-ren

we're English
somos ingleses
som-os eeng-glay-says

where are you from?
¿de dónde es usted?
day don-day es oos-ted

I'm 22
tengo veintidós
teng-goh bayn-tee-dos

are you a student?
¿eres estudiante?
ay-rays es-too-dyan-tay

I'm studying law
estudio derecho
es-too-dyoh day-rech-oh

I stay at home with the children
me quedo en casa con los niños
may kay-doh en ka-sa kon los neen-yohs

I work in marketing
trabajo en marketing
tra-ba-CHoh en mar-kay-teeng

I'm self-employed
soy autónomo
soy ow-toh-noh-moh

we don't have any children
no tenemos hijos
noh te-nay-mos ee-CHohs

two boys and a girl
dos niños y una niña
dos neen-yohs ee oo-na neen-ya

a boy of five and a girl of two
un niño de cinco años y una niña de dos
oon neen-yoh day seeng-koh an-yohs ee oo-na neen-ya day dos

have you ever been to to the United States/to Britain?
¿ha estado alguna vez en los Estados Unidos/en Gran Bretaña?
a es-tah-doh al-goo-na bes en los es-tah-dohs oo-nee-dohs/en gran bre-tan-ya

¿es usted estadounidense *or* **americano/inglés?**
are you American/English?

conozco Nueva York/Londres bastante bien
I know New York/London quite well

también estamos de vacaciones aquí
we're on *(Am)* vacation *or (Br)* holiday here too

me encantaría ir a California/Escocia algún día
I'd love to go to California/Scotland one day

tengo familia en los Estados Unidos/en Gran Bretaña
I have family in the States/in Britain

TALKING ABOUT YOUR STAY

Expressing yourself

I arrived three days ago
llegué hace tres días
yay-gay a-say trays dee-as

we've been here for a week
llevamos aquí una semana
yay-bah-mos a-kee a-say oo-na say-mah-na

I'm only here for the weekend
solo estoy aquí de fin de semana
soh-loh es-toy a-kee day feen day say-mah-na

we're just passing through
sólo estamos de paso
soh-loh es-tah-mos day pas-oh

this is our first time in...
ésta es la primera vez que venimos a...
es-ta es la pree-mair-a bes kay ben-ee-mos a...

I'm here on business
estoy aquí de negocios
es-toy a-kee day ne-goh-syohs

we're touring around
estamos visitando la zona
es-tah-mos bee-see-tan-doh la soh-na

we're on (Am) **vacation** or (Br) **holiday**
estamos de vacaciones
es-tah-mos day ba-kas-yoh-nays

we're here to celebrate our wedding anniversary
estamos aquí para celebrar nuestro aniversario de bodas
es-tah-mos a-kee pa-ra se-lay-brar nwes-troh a-nee-bair-sah-ryoh day boh-das

we're on our honeymoon
estamos de luna de miel
es-tah-mos day loo-na day myel

we're here with friends
estamos aquí con amigos
es-tah-mos a-kee kon a-mee-gohs

I've been told I should go to...
me han recomendado ir a...
may an rek-oh men dah doh eer a...

I'm planning to go to...
tengo pensado ir a...
teng-goh pen-suh-doh eer a...

Understanding

¡que le vaya bien!
enjoy your stay!

¡disfruten del resto de sus vacaciones!
enjoy the rest of your (Am) vacation or (Br) holiday!

¿es ésta la primera vez que viene a...?
is this your first time in...?

¿cuánto tiempo se va a quedar?
how long are you staying?

¿le gusta?
do you like it here?

¿ha estado en...?
have you been to...?

STAYING IN TOUCH

Expressing yourself

we should stay in touch
deberíamos seguir en contacto
de-bair-ee-a-mos se-geer en kon-tak-toh

I'll give you my e-mail address
le daré mi e-mail
lay dah-ray mee ee-mayl

here's my address, if you ever come to the States/to Britain
aquí tiene mi dirección, si alguna vez viene a los Estados Unidos/a
Gran Bretaña
a-kee tyen-ay mee dee-rek-syohn, see al-goo-na bes byen-ay a los es-tah-dohs oo-nee-dohs/a gran bre-tan-ya

Understanding

¿me dice su dirección?
will you give me your address?

¿tiene e-mail?
do you have an e-mail address?

puede venir a quedarse con nosotros cuando quiera
you're always welcome to come and stay with us here

EXPRESSING YOUR OPINION

Expressing yourself

I really like...
me gusta mucho...
may goos-ta moo-choh...

I really liked...
me gustó mucho...
may goos-toh moo-choh...

I don't like...
no me gusta...
noh may goos-ta...

I didn't like...
no me gustó...
noh may goos-toh...

I love...
me encanta...
may eng-kan-ta...

I loved...
me encantó...
may eng-kan-toh...

I would like...
me gustaría...
may goos-ta-ree-a...

I would have liked...
me habría gustado...
may a-bree-a goos-tah-doh...

I find it...
me parece...
may-pa-ray-say...

I found it...
me pareció...
may pa-ray-syoh...

it's great
es excelente *or (Arg, Mex)* genial *or (Carib)* chévere
es ek-say-len-tay/CHen-yahl/chay-bair-ay

it was great
fue excelente *or (Arg, Mex)* genial *or (Carib)* chévere
fway ek-say-len-tay/CHen-yahl/chay-bair-ay

it's not bad
no está mal
noh es-ta mal

it wasn't bad
no estuvo mal
noh es-too-boh mal

it's boring
es aburrido
es a-boo-RRee-doh

it was boring
fue aburrido
fway a-boo-RRee-doh

I agree
estoy de acuerdo
es-toy day a-kwair-doh

I don't agree
no estoy de acuerdo
noh es-toy day a-kwair-doh

I don't know
no sé
noh say

it doesn't appeal to me
no me hace mucha gracia
noh may a-say moo-cha gras-ya

it really annoys me
me molesta de verdad
may moh-les-ta day bair-dad

it's very quiet
está tranquilo
es-ta trang-kee-loh

it gets very busy at night
se llena de gente por la noche
say yay-na day CHen-tay por la no-chay

there was a really good atmosphere
había muy buen ambiente
a-bee-ya mwee bwen am-byen-tay

I really enjoyed myself
me lo pasé muy bien
may loh pa-say mwee byen

I didn't understand much
no he entendido mucho
noh ay en-ten-dee-doh moo-choh

we met some nice people
conocimos gente muy simpática
kon-oh-see-mos CHen-tay mwee sim-pa-tee-ka

we found a great hotel
encontramos un hotel muy bueno
eng-kon-trah-mos oon oh-tel mwee bway-noh

I don't mind
me da igual
may dah eeg-wahl

it sounds interesting
parece interesante
pa-re-say een-tay-ray-san-tay

it's a rip-off
es un robo
es oon roh-boh

it's too busy
hay demasiada gente
eye de-mas-yah-da CHen-tay

we had a great time
lo pasamos muy bien
loh pa-sah-mos mwee byen

Understanding

¿le gusta...?
do you like…?

¿quiere...?
would you like to…?

¿lo pasaron bien?
did you enjoy yourselves?

debería ir a...
you should go to…

no deje de probar...
you really must try...

no hay demasiados turistas
there aren't too many tourists

¿le gustó...?
did you like... ?

podríamos...
we could...

es una zona preciosa
it's a beautiful area

recomiendo...
I recommend…

merece or *(Arg)* **vale la pena**
it's worth it

no es tan bueno como dicen
it's a bit overrated

no vaya el fin de semana, hay demasiada gente
don't go on/at the weekend, it's too busy

TALKING ABOUT THE WEATHER

> **Some informal expressions**
>
> **hace un frío que pela** it's freezing cold
> **hace un tiempo de perros** the weather's foul
> **hace un calor agobiante** it's stifling

Expressing yourself

what's the weather forecast for tomorrow?
¿cuál es el pronóstico del tiempo para mañana?
kwal es el proh-nos-tee-koh del tyem-poh pa-ra man-yah-na

it's going to be nice
va a hacer buen tiempo
ba a a-sair bwen tyem-poh

it's not going to be nice
no va a hacer buen tiempo
noh ba a a-sair bwen tyem-poh

it's really hot
hace mucho calor
*a-say **moo**-choh ka-**lor***

it's really cold
hace mucho frío
*a-say **moo**-choh **free**-oh*

it gets cold at night
por la noche hace frío
*por la **no**-chay a-say **free**-oh*

the weather was beautiful
el tiempo estaba magnífico
*el **tyem**-poh es-**tah**-ba mag-**nee**-fee-koh*

it rained a few times
llovió algunas veces
*yoh-**byoh** al-**goo**-nas **bay**-says*

it was raining heavily
llovía mucho
*yoh-**bee**-a **moo**-choh*

there was a thunderstorm
hubo tormenta
*oo-boh tor-**men**-ta*

it's very humid here
hay mucha humedad aquí
*eye **moo**-cha oo-may-**dad** a-kee*

it's been lovely all week
ha hecho muy bueno toda la semana
*a e-choh mwee **bway**-noh **toh**-da la say-**mah**-na*

we've been lucky with the weather
hemos tenido suerte con el tiempo
*ay-mos te-**nee**-doh **swair**-tay kon el **tyem**-poh*

what a lovely day!
¡qué día tan bonito!
*kay **dee**-ya tan bon-**ee**-toh*

what awful weather!
¡qué asco de tiempo!
*kay **as**-koh day **tyem**-poh*

Understanding

dicen que va a llover
it's supposed to rain

mañana hará calor otra vez
it will be hot again tomorrow

han previsto buen tiempo para el resto de la semana
they've forecast good weather for the rest of the week

The basics

airport	aeropuerto *eye-roh-**pwair**-toh*
baggage room *(Am)*	consigna *kon-**seeg**-na*, *(Mex)* guardaequipajes ***gwar**-da-ek-ee-**pa**-CHays*
boarding	embarque *em-**bar**-kay*
boarding card	tarjeta de embarque *tar-**CHay**-ta day em-**bar**-kay*, *(Mex)* pase de abordar ***pa**-say day a-bor-**dar***
boat	barco ***bar**-koh*
bus	bus *boos*, *(Arg, Peru)* micro ***mee**-kroh*, *(Mex)* camión *kam-**yohn***
bus station	estación de buses or *(Arg, Peru)* micros or *(Mex)* camiones *es-tas-**yohn** day boo-**says**/**mee**-krohs/cam-**yohn**-ays*
bus stop	parada de *(Arg)* micros or *(Mex)* camiones *pa-**rah**-da day **mee**-krohs/kam-**yohn**-ays*, *(Peru)* paradero de micros *pa-ra-**dair**-oh day **mee**-krohs*
car	coche *ko-chay*, *(Arg)* auto ***ow**-toh*, *(Mex, Peru)* carro *ka-**RRoh***
check-in	registro *ray-**CHees**-troh*
city centre	centro de la ciudad *sen-troh day la syoo-**dad***
coach	*(bus)* bus *boos*, *(Arg)* micro ***mee**-kroh*, *(Mex)* camión foráneo *kam-**yohn** foh ra nay oh*, *(Peru)* bus interprovincial *boos een-tair-proh-been-**syahl***; *Br (on train)* vagón *ba-**gohn***, coche *ko-chay*
downtown *(Am)*	centro de la ciudad *sen-troh day la syoo-**dad***
ferry	ferry *fe-**RRee***, *(Mex)* buque *boo-kay*
flight	vuelo *bway-loh*
freeway *(Am)*	autopista *ow-toh-**pees**-ta*, *(Arg, Peru)* carretera *ka-**RRay**-**tair**-a*
gate	puerta ***pwair**-ta*
left-luggage (office) *(Br)*	consigna *kon-**seeg**-na*, *(Mex)* guardaequipajes ***gwar**-da-ek-ee-**pa**-CHays*

luggage	equipaje *ek-ee-pa-CHay*
map	mapa *ma-pa*
motorway *(Br)*	autopista *ow-toh-pees-ta*, *(Arg, Peru)* carretera *ka-RRay-tair-a*
one-way (ticket) *(Am)*	*(Arg, Peru)* pasaje de ida *pa-sa-CHay day ee-da*, *(Mex)* boleto sencillo *boh-lay-toh sen-see-yoh*
passport	pasaporte *pa-sa-por-tay*
plane	avión *ab-yohn*
platform	plataforma *pla-ta-for-ma*
railway station *(Br)*	estación de trenes *es-tas-yohn day tray-nes*
return (ticket)	*(Arg)* pasaje or *(Mex, Peru)* boleto de ida y vuelta *pa-sa-CHay/boh-lay-toh day ee-da ee bwel-ta*
road	carretera *ka-RRay-tair-a*
round-trip (ticket) *(Am)*	*(Arg)* pasaje or *(Mex, Peru)* boleto de ida y vuelta *pa-sa-CHay/boh-lay-toh day ee-da ee bwel-ta*
shuttle bus	*(Arg, Mex)* camioneta *kam-yohn-ay-ta*, *(Peru)* custer *koos-tair*
single (ticket) *(Br)*	*(Arg, Peru)* pasaje de ida *pa-sa-CHay day ee-da*, *(Mex)* boleto sencillo *boh-lay-toh sen-see-yoh*
street	calle *kal-yay*
streetcar *(Am)*	tranvía *tram-bee-a*
streetmap	mapa de calles *ma-pa day kal-yays*
subway *(Am)*	metro *may-troh*, *(Arg)* subte *soob-tay*
subway station *(Am)*	estación de metro or *(Arg)* subte *es-tas-yohn day may-troh/soob-tay*
taxi	taxi *tak-see*
terminal	terminal *tair-mee-nal*
ticket	billete *bee-yay-tay*, *(Arg)* pasaje *pa-sa-CHay*, *(Mex, Peru)* boleto *boh-lay-toh*
timetable	horario *aw-rah-ree-oh*
town centre *(Br)*	centro de la ciudad *sen-troh day la syoo-dad*
train	tren *trayn*
train station	estación de trenes *es-tas-yohn day tray-nes*
tram	tranvía *tram-bee-a*
underground *(Br)*	metro *may-troh*, *(Arg)* subte *soob-tay*

 GETTING AROUND

underground station (Br)	estación de metro or (Arg) subte *es-tas-yohn day may-troh*/**soob**-*tay*
to book	reservar *res-air-bar*
to hire	alquiler *al-kee-lair*
to rent	alquiler *al-kee-lair*
to reserve	reservar *res-air-bar*

Expressing yourself

where can I buy tickets?
¿dónde se compran los (Arg) pasajes or (Mex, Peru) boletos?
don-day say kom-pran los pa-sa-CHays/boh-lay-tohs

a ticket to..., please
un (Arg) pasaje or (Mex, Peru) boleto para..., por favor
oon pa-sa-CHay/boh-lay-toh pa-ra..., por fa-bor

I'd like to reserve or (Br) **book a ticket**
quisiera reservar un (Arg) pasaje or (Mex, Peru) boleto
kees-yair-a res-air-bar oon pa-sa-CHay/boh-lay-toh

how much is a ticket to...?
¿cuánto es un (Arg) pasaje or (Mex, Peru) boleto para...?
kwan-toh es oon pa-sa-CHay/boh-lay-toh pa-ra...

are there any student discounts?
¿hay descuentos para estudiantes?
eye des-kwen-tohs pa-ra es-too-dyan-tays

could I have a timetable, please?
¿me da un horario, por favor?
may dah oon aw-rah-ree-oh, por fa-bor

are there any seats left for...?
¿le quedan asientos para...?
lay kay-dan as-yen-tohs pa-ra...

is there an earlier/later one?
¿hay uno más temprano/más tarde?
eye oo-noh mas tem-prah-noh/mas tar-day

how long is the trip?
¿cuánto dura el viaje?
kwan-toh doo-ra el bee-a-CHay

is this seat free?
¿está libre este asiento?
es-ta lee-bray es-tay a-syen-toh

I'm sorry, there's someone sitting there
lo siento, está ocupado
loh syen-toh, es-ta o-koo-pah-doh

Understanding

atrasado	delayed
baños	(Am) restrooms, (Br) toilets
boletos	tickets
caballeros	(Am) men's room, (Br) gents
cancelado	cancelled
conexiones	connections
damas	(Am) ladies' room, (Br) ladies
entrada	entrance
hombres	(Am) men's room, (Br) gents
información	information
llegadas	arrivals
pasajes	tickets
prohibida la entrada	no entry
retrasado	delayed
salida	exit
salidas	departures
señoras	(Am) ladies' room, (Br) ladies

todos los (Arg) **pasajes** or (Mex, Peru) **boletos están agotados**
everything is fully booked

BY PLANE

Understanding

where's the American Airlines check-in?
¿dónde está el mostrador de American Airlines?
don-day es-ta el mos-tra-dor day a-mair-ee-kan air-leynes

I have an e-ticket
tengo un (Arg) **pasaje** or (Mex, Peru) **boleto electrónico**
teng-goh oon pa-sa-CHay/boh-lay-toh ay-lek-tron-ee-koh

one suitcase and one piece of hand luggage
una *(Arg)* valija *or (Mex, Peru)* maleta y un *(Arg)* bolso *or (Peru)* maletín *or (Mex)* una maleta de mano
oo-na ba-*lee*-CHa/ma-*lay*-ta ee oon *bol*-soh/ma-lay-*teen*/oo-na ma-*lay*-ta day *mah*-noh

what time do we board?
¿a qué hora embarcamos?
a kay *aw*-ra em-bar-*kah*-mos

I'd like to confirm my return flight
quisiera confirmar el vuelo de vuelta
kees-*yair*-a kon-feer-*mar* el *bway*-loh day *bwel*-ta

one of my suitcases is missing
me falta una de mis *(Arg)* valijas *or (Mex, Peru)* maletas
may *fal*-ta *oo*-na day mees ba-*lee*-CHas/ma-*lay*-tas

my luggage hasn't arrived
mi equipaje no ha llegado
mee ek-ee-*pa*-CHay noh a yay-*gah*-doh

the plane was two hours late
el avión se retrasó dos horas
el ab-*yohn* say re-tra-*soh* dos *aw*-ras

I've missed my connection
he perdido la conexión
ay pair-*dee*-doh mee ko-neks-*yohn*

I've left something on the plane
he olvidado una cosa en el avión
ay ol-bee-*dah*-doh *oo*-na *koh*-sa en el ab-*yohn*

I want to report the loss of my luggage
quiero denunciar la pérdida de mi equipaje
kyair-oh day-noon-*syar* la *pair*-dee-da day mee ek-ee-*pa*-CHay

Understanding

aduana	customs
algo que declarar	goods to declare
control de pasaportes	passport control
embarque inmediato	immediate boarding
nada que declarar	nothing to declare

recogida or (Mex) **reclamación de equipaje**	(Am) baggage claim, (Br) baggage reclaim
registro	check-in
sala de embarque	departure lounge
vuelos nacionales	domestic flights

por favor, espere en la sala de embarque
please wait in the departure lounge

¿quiere un siento de ventana o pasillo?
would you like a window seat or an aisle seat?

tendrá que hacer transbordo en…
you'll have to change in…

¿cuántas (Arg) valijas or (Mex, Peru) maletas tiene?
how many bags do you have?

¿ha hecho usted mismo las (Arg) valijas or (Mex, Peru) maletas?
did you pack all your bags yourself?

¿le ha dado alguien algo para llevar?
has anyone given you anything to take on board?

tiene un exceso de equipaje de diez kilos
your luggage is ten kilos overweight

aquí tiene la tarjeta de embarque or (Mex) el pase de abordar
here's your boarding card

el embarque empezará a las…
boarding will begin at...

por favor diríjase a la puerta número…
please proceed to gate number…

última llamada para…
this is a final call for…

puede llamar a este número para ver si su equipaje ha llegado
you can call this number to check that your luggage has arrived

BY TRAIN, COACH, BUS, SUBWAY

In Latin America, trains are mainly used to transport goods. Passenger trains tend to be slow and not very comfortable. There are exceptions, though, particularly for short distances such as the Cuzco – Aguas Calientes route in Peru, which is popular with tourists travelling to Machu Picchu.

The most common way to get around, including for long journeys, is by coach. These are generally modern, fast and comfortable, although the state of the roads can vary according to the area.

If you're travelling in a group, it's worth finding out about the price of taxis, as it's usually quite cheap to share one. Taxis are more comfortable than buses and have the advantage of being safe from pickpockets.

Mexico City, Buenos Aires and Caracas all have subway systems. These are in good condition and provide a safe and comfortable way to travel.

Expressing yourself

can I have *(Am)* **a subway map** *or (Br)* **a map of the underground, please?**
¿me da un mapa del metro *or (Arg)* subte?
*may dah oon **ma**-pa del **may**-troh/**soob**-tay*

what time is the next train to...?
¿a qué hora es el próximo tren para...?
*a kay **aw**-ra es el **prok**-see-moh trayn **pa**-ra...*

what time is the last train?
¿a qué hora es el último tren?
*a kay **aw**-ra es el **ool**-tee-moh trayn*

which platform is it for...?
¿de qué andén sale el tren a...?
*day kay an-**den sah**-lay el trayn a...*

where can I catch a bus to...?
¿dónde puedo tomar un bus *or (Arg, Peru)* micro *or (Mex)* camión ara...?
*don-day **pway**-doh toh-**mar** oon boos/**mee**-kroh/kam-**yohn pa**-ra...*

which line do I take to get to...?
¿cuál es la línea para ir a...?
kwal es la lee-nay-a pa-ra eer a...

is this the stop for...?
¿ésta es la parada *or (Peru)* el paradero de...?
es-ta es la pa-rah-da/el pa-rah-dair-oh day...

is this where the coach leaves for...?
¿de aquí sale el bus *or (Arg)* micro *or (Mex)* camión foráneo *or (Peru)*
   bus interprovincial para...?
*day a-kee sa-lay el boos/mee-kroh/kam-yohn foh-rah-nay-oh/boos een-tair-
   proh-been-syahl pa-ra...*

can you tell me when I need to get off?
¿puede decirme dónde tengo que bajarme?
pway-day de-seer-may don-day teng-goh kay ba-CHar-may

I've missed my train/bus
he perdido el tren/bus *or (Arg, Peru)* micro *or (Mex)* camión
ay pair-dee-doh el trayn/boos/mee-kroh/kam-yohn

Understanding

acceso a los andenes	to the trains
boletería	ticket office
boletos internet	e-tickets
mensual	monthly
pasajes internet	e-tickets
reservas	reservations
salida immediata	tickets for travel today
salidas diarias	daily departures
semanal	weekly
transbordo	change, connection
venta anticipada	advance booking
venta anticipada Internet	Internet bookings

hay una parada *or (Peru)* **un paradero un poco más adelante a la
   derecha**
there's a stop a bit further along on the right

sólo precio exacto, por favor
exact change *or* money only, please

tendrá que hacer transbordo en…
you'll have to change at…

tiene que tomar el bus *or (Arg, Peru)* **micro** *or (Mex)* **camión número…**
you need to get the number… bus

el tren tiene parada *or (Peru)* **paradero en…**
this train stops *or (Br)* calls at…

a dos paradas *or (Peru)* **paraderos de aquí**
two stops from here

BY CAR

Latin America has a reasonable road network. Most motorways have tolls, and the speed limit is between 100 and 120 km/h on motorways and highways, while in cities it is 60 km/h. You can buy lead-free petrol and diesel at service stations, where it is customary to tip. In rural areas it's best to check road conditions before travel. To reduce pollution in Mexico City, there are restrictions on car use based on the last digit of the vehicle licence plate. In Mexico City and Buenos Aires the best way to get around is by subway. Taxis generally have meters – if yours does not, agree on a price before you set off. Some taxi companies offer prepaid rides at fixed prices from airports and bus/train stations. They usually charge a supplement for luggage, as well as on Sundays and holidays and at night.

Expressing yourself

where can I find a service station?
¿dónde hay una estación de servicio *or (Mex)* gasolinería *or (Peru)* un grifo?
don-day eye **oo**-*na es-tas-***yohn** *day sair-***bees**-*yoh/gas-oh-lee-nair-***ee**-*a/ oon* **gree**-*foh*

lead-free *(Am)* **gas** *or (Br)* **petrol, please**
gasolina *or (Arg)* nafta sin plomo, por favor
gas-oh-lee-na/naf-ta seen ploh-moh, por fa-bor

how much is it per litre?
¿a cuánto está el litro?
a kwan-toh es-ta el lee-troh

we got stuck in a traffic jam
nos quedamos parados en un *(Arg)* embotellamiento *or (Mex)* atasco
or (Peru) atolladero
nos kay-dah-mos pa-rah-dohs en oon em-boh-tay-a-myen-toh/a-tas-koh/a-toh-ya-dair-oh

is there a garage near here?
¿hay un taller mecánico por aquí?
eye oon ta-yair may-kan-ee-koh por a-kee

can you help us push the car?
¿nos ayuda a empujar el coche *or (Arg)* auto *or (Mex, Peru)* carro?
nos a-yoo-da a em-poo-CHar el ko-chay/ow-toh/ka-RRoh

the battery's dead	**my car's broken down**
se ha descargado la batería	tengo una avería
say a des-kar-gah-doh la ba-tair-ee-a	*teng-goh oo-na a-bair-ee-a*

we've run out of *(Am)* **gas** *or (Br)* **petrol**
nos quedamos sin gasolina *or (Arg)* nafta
nos kay-dah-mos seen gas-oh-lee-na/naf-ta

I've got a puncture and my spare tyre is flat
se me pinchó *or (Mex)* ponchó una llanta y tengo la *(Arg)* rueda auxiliar
or (Mex) llanta de refacción *or (Peru)* repuesto desinflada
say may peen-cho/pon-cho oo-na yan-ta ee teng-goh la rway-da awk-see-lyar/yan-ta day ray-fak-syohn/ray-pwes-toh des-in-flah-da

we've had an accident
hemos tenido un accidente
ay-mos te-nee-doh oon ak-see-den-tay

I've lost my car keys
he perdido las llaves de mi coche *or (Arg)* auto *(or Mex, Peru)* carro
ay pair-dee-doh las yah-bays day mee ko-chay/ow-toh/ka-RRoh

how long will it take to repair?
¿cuánto tardará en arreglarlo?
kwan-toh tar-da-rah en a-RRay-glar-loh

◆ Renting a car

I'd like to rent a car for a week
quisiera alquilar un coche or *(Arg)* auto or *(Mex, Peru)* carro por una semana
kees-yair-a al-kee-lar oon ko-chay/ow-toh/ka-RRoh por oo-na say-mah-na

an automatic (car)
un coche or *(Arg)* auto or *(Mex, Peru)* carro automático
oon ko-chay/ow-toh/ka-RRoh ow-toh-ma-tee-koh

I'd like to take out comprehensive insurance
quisiera un seguro a or *(Arg)* contra todo riesgo or *(Mex)* de cobertura total
kees-yair-a oon say-goo-roh a/kon-tra toh-doh ree-es-goh/day koh-bair-too-rah toh-tahl

◆ Getting a taxi

is there *(Am)* a taxi stand or *(Br)* a taxi rank near here?
¿hay una parada or *(Mex)* un sitio de taxis por aquí?
eye oo-na pa-rah-da/un see-tyoh day tak-sees por a-kee

I'd like to go to…
quisiera ir a…
kees-yair-a eer a…

I'd like a taxi for 8 p.m.
quisiera reservar un taxi para las ocho de la noche
kees-yair-a re-sair-bar oon tak-see pa-ra las o-choh day la no-chay

you can drop me off here, thanks
puede dejarme aquí, gracias
pway-day day-CHar-may a-kee, gras-yas

how much will it be to go to the airport?
¿cuánto cuesta ir al aeropuerto?
kwan-toh kwes-ta eer al eye-roh-pwair-toh

◆ Hitchhiking

I'm going to…
voy a…
boy a…

can you drop me off here?
¿puede dejarme aquí?
pway-day day-CHar-may a-kee

could you take me as far as…?
¿puede llevarme hasta…?
pway-day yay-bar-may as-ta…

thanks for the *(Am)* **ride** or *(Br)* **lift**
gracias por el viaje
gras-yas por el bee-a-CHay

we hitched *(Am)* **a ride** or *(Br)* **a lift**
(Arg) fuimos a dedo, *(Mex)* viajamos de aventón, *(Peru)* tiramos dedo
fwee-mos a day-doh/bee-ah-CHa-mohs day a-ben-tohn/tee-rah-mos day-doh

---

Understanding

alquiler de coches or *(Arg)* **autos** or *(Mex, Peru)* **carros**	car rental
conserve su *(Arg, Peru)* **ticket** or *(Mex)* **boleto**	keep your ticket
estacionamiento	*(Am)* parking lot, *(Br)* car park
libre	spaces *(for parking)*
lleno	full *(no parking spaces)*
otras direcciones	other directions
prohibido estacionar	no parking
reduzca velocidad	slow
todas direcciones	all directions

necesito su carnet or *(Mex)* **licencia de conducir** or *(Peru)* **brevete, documento de identidad, y su tarjeta de crédito**
I'll need your *(Am)* driver's license or *(Br)* driving licence, proof of identity and your credit card

hay una fianza or *(Arg, Peru)* **garantía de 1000 pesos**
there's a 1000-peso deposit

BY BOAT

Argentina and Uruguay are connected by ferry; **Buquebus** provides four daily services linking Buenos Aires to Montevideo.

Expressing yourself

how long is the crossing?
¿cuánto dura la travesía?
kwan-toh doo-ra la tra-be-see-a

I'm seasick
estoy mareado
es-toy ma-ray-ah-doh

Understanding

sólo pasajeros de a pie *(Am)* passengers without a car *or (Br)* foot
   passengers only
proxima salida a las... next sailing at...

ACCOMMODATION

There are various accommodation options throughout Latin America, but it is best to book ahead, particularly during high season. Online booking is still relatively rare. **Hostales** and **albergues** (these are essentially the same, that is small, family-run guest houses) are a good budget option. However, prices can vary considerably depending on the season, and may double or even triple in high season. Quality varies too, so make sure you ask to see your room before you accept it. At reception, you'll be asked for some ID and may be required to fill out a form. Hotels (**hoteles**) are more expensive and reservations are essential in high season. Hotel and restaurant charges include tax (called **IVA** in Argentina and Mexico, **IGV** in Peru), which varies between 15% and 20%.

The basics

all-inclusive	todo incluido *toh*-doh eeng-kloo-**ee**-doh
American plan *(Am)*	pensión completa pen-**syohn** kom-**play**-ta
apartment	apartamento a-par-ta-**men**-toh, departamento day-par-ta-**men**-toh
bath	baño ban-yoh
bathroom	cuarto de baño kwar-toh day ban-yoh
bathtub *(Am)*	bañera ban-**yair**-a
bed	cama ka-ma
bed and breakfast	pensión pen-**syohn**, hostal os-**tahl**, *(Carib)* parador pa-ra-**dor**
cable television	televisión por cable te-lay-bees-**yohn** por kab-lay
campsite	camping **kam**-ping
caravan	casa *(Arg)* rodante or *(Mex)* sobre ruedas ka-sa ro-**dahn**-tay/so-bray **rway**-das, *(Carib)* trailer **treye**-ler, *(Peru)* carro-casa ka-**RRo** ka-sa
cottage	casa de campo ka-sa day **cam**-poh
double bed	cama doble ka-ma **doh**-blay
double room	habitación doble a-bee-tas-**yohn doh**-blay

en-suite bathroom *(Br)*	habitación con baño *a-bee-tas-yohn* kon *ban-yoh*
family room *(Br)*	habitación familiar *a-bee-tas-yohn* fa-meel-*yar*
flat *(Br)*	apartamento *a-par-ta-men-toh*, departamento *day-par-ta-men-toh*
full board *(Br)*	pensión completa *pen-syohn* kom-*play-ta*
half board *(Br)*	media pensión *med-ya pen-syohn*
hotel	hotel *oh-tel*
key	llave *ya-bay*
modified American plan *(Am)*	media pensión *med-ya pen-syohn*
rent *(noun)*	alquiler *al-kee-lair*
restrooms *(Am)*	baños *ban-yohs*
satellite television	televisión por satélite *te-lay-bees-yohn* por *sa-tay-lee-tay*
self-catering *(Br)*	con cocina propia kon ko-*see*-na proh-pee-ya
shower	ducha *doo-cha*
single bed	cama individual *ka-ma* een-dee-bee-*dwal*
single room	habitación individual *a-bee-tas-yohn* een-dee-bee-*dwal*
tenant	inquilino *een-kee-lee-noh*
tent	*(Arg, Peru)* carpa *kar-pa*, *(Carib)* caseta (de campaña) *ka-say-ta day kam-pan-ya*, *(Mex)* tienda *tyen-da*
toilets *(Br)*	baños *ban-yohs*
trailer *(Am)*	casa *(Arg)* rodante or *(Mex)* sobre ruedas *ka-sa* ro-*dahn-tay*/so-bray *rway-das*, *(Carib)* trailer *treye-ler*, *(Peru)* carro-casa *ka-RRo ka-sa*
youth hostel	albergue juvenil *al-bair-gay* CHoo-bay-*neel*
to book *(Br)*	reservar *re-sair-bar*
to rent	alquilar *al-kee-lar*
to reserve	reservar *re-sair-bar*

Expressing yourself

I have a reservation
tengo una reserva
teng-goh oo-na re-sair-ba

the name's…
a nombre de…
a nom-bray day…

do you take credit cards?
¿aceptan tarjetas de crédito?
a-sep-tan tar-CHay-tas day kred-ee-toh

Understanding

completo	full
habitación con baño	room with a bathroom
habitación doble	double room
habitación individual	single room
habitaciones libres	vacancies
lleno	full
privado	private
recepción	reception, front desk

¿me permite su pasaporte, por favor?
could I see your passport, please?

¿puede rellenar este formulario or *(Mex)* **esta forma?**
could you fill out this form?

HOTELS

Expressing yourself

do you have any vacancies?
¿tienen habitaciones libres?
tyen-en a-bee-tas-yoh-nays lee-brays

how much is a double/single room per night?
¿cuánto es una habitación doble/individual por noche?
kwan-toh es oo-na a-bee-tas-yohn doh-blay/een-dee-bee-dwal por no-chay

I'd like to reserve a double/single room
quisiera reservar una habitación doble/individual
kees-*yair*-a re-sair-*var* oo-na a-bee-tas-*yohn* doh-blay/een-dee-bee-*dwal*

for three nights
para tres noches
pa-ra trays *no*-chays

would it be possible to stay an extra night?
¿podría quedarme una noche más?
pod-*ree*-a kay-*dar*-may oo-na *no*-chay mas

do you have any rooms available for tonight?
¿tienen habitaciones para esta noche?
tyen-en a-bee-tas-*yoh*-nays *pa*-ra *es*-ta *no*-chay

do you have any family rooms?
¿tienen habitaciones familiares?
tyen-en a-bee-tas-*yoh*-nays fa-meel-*yah*-rays

would it be possible to add an extra bed?
¿podrían poner una cama extra?
pod-*ree*-an pon-*air* oo-na *ka*-ma *ex*-tra

could I see the room first?
¿podría ver la habitación primero?
pod-*ree*-a bair la a-bee-tas-*yohn* pree-*mair*-oh

do you have anything bigger/quieter?
¿tiene algo más grande/tranquilo?
tyen-ay *al*-goh mas *gran*-day/trang-*kee*-loh

could you recommend any other hotels?
¿podría recomendarme otros hoteles?
pod-*ree*-a re-kom-en-*dar*-may *oh*-trohs oh-*tel*-ays

is breakfast included?
¿está incluido el desayuno?
es-*ta* eeng-kloo-*ee*-doh el des-eye-oo-noh

that's fine, I'll take it
está bien, me la quedo
es-*ta* byen, may la *kay*-doh

what time do you serve breakfast?
¿a qué hora sirven el desayuno?
a kay *aw*-ra *seer*-ben el des-eye-*oo*-noh

is there *(Am)* **an elevator** *or (Br)* **a lift?**
¿hay ascensor?
*eye as-sen-**sor***

is the hotel near the city centre?
¿el hotel está cerca del centro?
*el oh-**tel** es-**ta** **sair**-ka del **sen**-troh*

what time will the room be ready?
¿a qué hora estará lista la habitación?
*a kay **aw**-ra es-ta-**ra lees**-ta la a-bee-tas-**yohn***

the key for room…, please
la llave para la habitación…, por favor
*la **yah**-bay **pa**-ra la a-bee-tas-**yohn**… por fa-**bor***

could I have an extra blanket?
¿puede darme una manta *or* frazada *or* *((Carib)* colcha *or (Mex)* cobija más?
*pway-day **dar**-may oo-na **man**-ta/fra-**sa**-da/**kol**-cha/ko-**bee**-CHa mas*

the air conditioning isn't working
el aire acondicionado no funciona
*el **eye**-ray a-kon-dees-yon-**ah**-doh noh foon-**syoh**-na*

Understanding

lo siento, estamos
I'm sorry, but we're full

¿para cuántas noches es?
how many nights is it for?

sólo tenemos libre una habitación *or* **un cuarto individual**
we only have a single room available

¿su nombre, por favor?
what's your name, please?

pueden entrar a partir del mediodía
check-in is from midday

tiene que dejar la habitación *or* **el cuarto antes de las 11 de la mañana**
you have to check out before 11 a.m.

ACCOMMODATION

el desayuno se sirve en el restaurante entre 7:30 y 9:00
breakfast is served in the restaurant between 7:30 and 9:00

¿quiere un periódico or **diario por la mañana?**
would you like a newspaper in the morning?

su habitación no está lista todavía
your room isn't ready yet

puede dejar sus maletas or (Arg) **valijas aquí**
you can leave your bags here

YOUTH HOSTELS

Some youth hostels (**albergues juveniles**) in Latin America impose a
curfew. They are not much cheaper than guest houses (**pensiones**).

Expressing yourself

do you have space for two people for tonight?
¿tiene sitio or lugar para dos personas para esta noche?
*tyen-ay **seet**-yoh/loo-**gar** pa-ra dos pair-**soh**-nas pa-ra es-ta **no**-chay*

we've reserved two beds for three nights
hemos reservado dos camas para tres noches
*ay-mos re-sair-**bah**-doh dos **ka**-mas pa-ra trays **no**-chays*

could I leave my backpack at (Am) **the front desk** or (Br) **reception?**
¿puedo dejar mi mochila en recepción or (Cuba) carpeta?
***pway**-doh day-**CHar** mee moh-**chee**-la en ray-sep-**syohn**/kar-**pay**-ta*

do you have somewhere we could leave our bikes?
¿hay algún sitio para dejar las bicicletas?
*eye al-**goon seet**-yoh pa-ra day-**CHar** las bee-see-**klay**-tas*

I'll come back for it around 7 o'clock
volveré a recogerlo a las 7
*bol-bair-**ay** a re-koh-**CHair**-loh a las **sye**-tay*

there's no hot water
no hay agua caliente
*noh eye **ag**-wa kal-**yen**-tay*

the sink's blocked up
el lavabo está atascado or *(Mex)* tapado, *(Arg)* la pileta está tapada,
  (Carib) el lavamanos está tapado, *(Peru)* el lavatorio está atorado
*el la-**bah**-boh es-**ta** a-tas-**kah**-doh/ta-**pah**-doh/la pee-**lay**-ta es-**ta** ta-**pah**-da/el
  la-bah-**mah**-nos es-**ta** ta-**pah**-doh/el la-ba-**taw**-ree-oh es-**ta** a-taw-**ra**-doh*

Understanding

¿tienes tarjeta de socio?
do you have a membership card?

se proporciona la ropa de cama
bed linen is provided

el albergue vuelve a abrir a las 6
the hostel reopens at 6 p.m.

SELF-CATERING

Expressing yourself

we're looking for somewhere to rent near a city/town
buscamos algo para alquilar cerca de una ciudad
*boos-**kah**-mos al-goh pa-ra al-kee-**lar** sair-ka day la syoo-**dad***

where do we pick up/leave the keys?
¿dónde recogemos/dejamos las llaves?
***don**-day re-ko-**CHay**-mos/day-**CHah**-mos las **yah**-bays*

is electricity included in the price?
¿la electricidad está incluida en el precio?
*la el-ek-tree-see-**dad** es-**ta** eeng-kloo-**ee**-dah en el **pray**-syoh*

are bed linen and towels provided?
¿proporcionan las toallas y la ropa de cama?
*pro-por-**syoh**-nan las toh-**eye**-as ee la **roh**-pa day **ka**-ma*

do you need to have a car?
¿hace falta un coche *or (Arg)* auto *or (Carib, Mex, Peru)* carro?
a-say fal-ta oon ko-chay/ow-to/ka-RRo

is there a pool?
¿hay piscina *or (Mex)* alberca?
eye pee-see-na/al-bair-kah

is it suitable for elderly people?
¿está adaptado para personas mayores?
es-ta a-dap-tah-doh pa-ra pair-soh-nas meye-aw-rays

where is the nearest supermarket?
¿dónde está el supermercado más cercano?
don-day es-ta el soo-pair-mair-kah-doh mas sair-kah-noh

Understanding

por favor deje la casa ordenada y limpia antes de salir
please leave the house clean and tidy when you leave

la casa está totalmente amueblada
the house is fully furnished

el precio incluye todo
everything is included in the price

necesitas un coche *or (Arg)* **auto** *or (Carib, Mex, Peru)* **carro en esta parte del país**
you need a car in this part of the country

CAMPING

In Latin America, it is advisable to ask in tourist information offices about legal and safe sites for camping. Some campsites have facilities such as a supermarket, a restaurant and so on.

Expressing yourself

is there a campsite near here?
¿hay un camping por aquí cerca?
*eye oon **kam**-peeng por a-**kee sair**-ka*

I'd like to reserve a space for a tent for three nights
quiero reservar un espacio para una tienda *or (Arg, Peru)* carpa *or*
 (Carib) caseta (de campaña) para tres noches
*kyair-oh re-sair-**bar** oon es-**pas**-yoh **pa**-ra **oo**-na **tyen**-da/**kar**-pa/ka-**say**-ta
 (day kam-**pan**-ya) **pa**-ra trays no-chays*

how much is it a night?   **where are the showers?**
¿cuánto es por noche?   ¿dónde están las duchas?
kwan-toh es por no-chay   *don-day es-tan las doo-chas*

can we pay, please? we were at space…
¿podemos pagar? estamos en el espacio…
*pod-ay-mos pa-**gar**. es-**tah**-mos en el es-**pas**-yoh…*

Understanding

son… al día/por persona por noche/por tienda
it's… per day/per person per night/per tent

si necesita algo no dude en preguntar
if you need anything, just come and ask

EATING AND DRINKING

In cafés in Mexico ask for **café americano**, and in Argentina and Peru for a **café** if you want espresso, and for **café con leche** if you want it with milk. A **cortado** is an espresso with a dash of milk, and a **descafeinado** is a decaf. In Mexico, **café de olla** is made in a clay pot and served with cinnamon and sugar. Restaurants usually serve lunch between noon and 4 p.m., and dinner from 8:30 to 11:30 p.m., although in Mexico you can often dine earlier. Water and bread are not always included in the price. Tax (**IVA**) is included in the bill (between 12% and 20%, varying from one country to another). It is customary to leave 10% or at least a few coins as a tip, even if service is included. In Mexico there are no service charges.

If you want to go for a drink (**ir a tomar algo**) and to eat a light snack (**ir a comer algo**), bars are open from noon or earlier until late into the night. For draught beer, ask for **una jarra** or **un chop** in Argentina and Peru, **cerveza de barril** in the Caribbean or **un shot** in Mexico; for bottled beer, ask for **una cerveza**. **Una clara** is a shandy in Peru and **un vino** is a glass of wine (**vino blanco** is white wine, **vino tinto** is red). Most Mexican **taquerías** (snack bars specializing in tacos) do not sell alcohol, just **refrescos** (soft drinks) and **aguas frescas** (**jamaica, horchata, tamarindo**), which are flavoured, fruit-based drinks. In Cuba try the local **mojitos** (cocktails made with rum, lemon and mint).

In Cuba, besides restaurants there are **paladares**, an excellent budget option where homemade cooking is served in a family's dining room.

The basics

appetizer	entrada en-**trah**-da, (Carib) aperitivo a-pay-ree-**tee**-bo
beer	(bottled) cerveza sair-**bay**-sah
bill (Br)	cuenta kwen-ta
black coffee	café ka-**fay**
bottle	botella boh-**tay**-ya
bread	pan pan
breakfast	desayuno des-eye-**oo**-noh

check *(Am)*	cuenta *kwen-ta*
coffee	café *ka-fay*
coffee with milk	café con leche *ka-fay kon le-chay*
Coke®	Coca Cola® *koh-ka koh-la*
dessert	postre *pos-tray*
dinner	cena *say-na*
draught beer	*(Arg, Peru)* jarra *CHa-RRa*, chop *shop*, *(Carib)* cerveza de barril *sair-bay-sah day ba-RReel*, *(Mex)* shot *shot*
fruit juice	jugo de fruta *CHoo-goh day froo-ta*
lemonade	gaseosa *gas-ay-oh-sa*, *(Carib)* refresco *ray-frcs ko*, *(Mex)* limonada *lee-moh-nah-da*
lunch	almuerzo *al-mwair-soh*
main course	plato principal *plah-toh preen-see-pahl*
menu	menú *men-oo*
mineral water	agua mineral *ag-wa mee-nay-rahl*
red wine	vino tinto *bee-noh teen-toh*
rosé wine	vino rosado *bee-noh ro-sah-doh*
salad	ensalada *en-sa-lah-da*
sandwich	sandwich *san-weech*, *(Mex)* torta *tor-ta*
sparkling water	agua con gas *ag-wa kon gas*
sparkling wine	vino espumoso *bee-noh es-poo-moh-soh*
starter	entrada *en-trah-da*, *(Carib)* aperitivo *a-pay-ree-tee-boh*
still water *(Br)*	agua sin gas *ag-wa seen gas*
tea	té *tay*
tip	propina *proh-pee-na*
water	agua *ag-wa*
white wine	vino blanco *bee-noh blang-koh*
wine	vino *bee-noh*
wine list	lista de vinos *lees-ta day bee-nohs*
to eat	comer *kom-air*
to have breakfast	desayunar *des-eye-oo-nar*
to have dinner	cenar *say-nar*
to have lunch	almorzar *al-mor-sar*
to order	pedir *ped-eer*

EAT NG AND DRINKING

Expressing yourself

shall we go and have something to eat?
¿vamos a comer algo?
bah-mos a kom-air al-goh

do you want to go for a drink?
¿quieres ir a tomar *or* beber algo?
kyair-es eer a toh-mar/be-bair al-goh

can you recommend a good restaurant?
¿me recomienda un buen restaurante?
may ray-kom-yen-da oon bwen res-tow-ran-tay

I'm not very hungry
no tengo mucha hambre
noh teng-goh moo-cha am-bray

I'm starving
me muero de hambre
may mwair-oh day am-bray

excuse me! *(to call the waiter)*
(Arg, Peru) ¡mozo!, *(Carib, Mex)* ¡mesero!, ¡camarero!
moh-soh/may-sair-oh/ka-ma-rair-oh

I'll have the same again
tomaré otro
toh-mah-ray oh-troh

cheers!
¡salud!
sa-lood

that was lovely
estaba muy rico
es-tah-ba mwee ree-koh

could you bring us an ashtray, please?
¿puede traernos un cenicero, por favor?
pway-day tra-air-nos oon sen-ee-sair-oh, por fa-bor

where are the *(Am)* **restrooms** *or (Br)* **toilets, please?**
¿dónde están los baños?
don-day es-tan los ban-yohs

Understanding

comida para llevar   *(Am)* takeout, *(Br)* takeaway

lo siento, dejamos de servir a las 11
I'm sorry, we stop serving at 11 p.m.

RESERVING A TABLE

Expressing yourself

I'd like to reserve a table for tomorrow evening
quiero reservar una mesa para mañana *(Arg)* a *or (Carib, Mex)* por *or (Peru)* en la noche
kyair-oh res-air-bar oo-na may-sa pa-ra man-yah-na a/por/en la no-chay

for two people
para dos personas
pa-ra dos pair-soh-nas

around 8 o'clock
alrededor de *or* cerca de *or* sobre las ocho
al-ray-day-dor day/sair-ka day/soh-bray las o-choh

do you have a table available any earlier than that?
¿tiene una mesa libre más temprano?
tyen-ay oo-na may-sa lee-bray mas tem-prah-noh

I've reserved a table – the name's…
he reservado una mesa a nombre de…
ay res-air-bah-doh oo-na may-sa a nom-bray day…

a table for four, please
una mesa para cuatro, por favor
oo-na may-sa pa-ra kwat-roh, por fa-bor

Understanding

reservado

reserved

¿para qué hora?
for what time?

¿para cuántas personas?
for how many people?

¿tiene reserva?
do you have a reservation?

¿a qué nombre?
what's the name?

¿fumador o no fumador?
smoking or non-smoking?

lo siento, no nos quedan mesas libres
I'm afraid we're full at the moment

ORDERING FOOD

Expressing yourself

yes, we're ready to order
sí, ya hemos elegido
see, ya *ay*-mos el-ay-*CHee*-doh

no, could you give us a few more minutes?
no, ¿puede darnos un momentito más?
noh, *pway*-day *dar*-nos oon moh-men-*tee*-toh mas

what do you recommend?
¿qué nos recomienda?
kay nos ray-kom-*yen*-da

I'll have that
voy a pedir eso
boy a ped-*eer* es-oh

I'd like...
quiero...
kyair-oh...

could I have...?
¿me trae...? or ¿me puede traer...?
may *tra*-ay/may *pway*-day tra-*air*

I'm not sure, what's cebiche?
no sé, ¿qué es el cebiche?
noh say, kay es el say-*bee*-chay

does it come with vegetables?
¿viene con verduras?
byen-ay kon bair-*doo*-ras

what are today's specials?
¿cuál es la especialidad del día?
kwal es la es-pes-ya-lee-*dad* del *dee*-a

what desserts do you have?
¿qué postres tiene?
kay *pos*-trays *tyen*-ay

I'm vegetarian
soy vegetariano/a
soy be-*CHay*-tah-ree-*ah*-noh/be-*CHay*-tah-ree-*ah*-na

a bottle of red/white wine
una botella de vino tinto/blanco
*oo-na bo-**tel**-ya day **bee**-noh **blang**-koh/**teen**-toh*

some water, please
agua, por favor
*ag-wa, por fa-**bor***

that's for me
eso es para mí
*es-oh es **pa**-ra mee*

this isn't what I ordered, I wanted…
esto no es lo que he pedido, yo quería…
*es-toh noh es loh kay ay pe-**dee**-doh, yoh kair-ee-a…*

could we have some more bread, please?
¿puede traernos más pan, por favor?
*pway-day tra-**air**-nos mas pan, por fa-**bor***

could we have another *(Am)* **pitcher** or *(Br)* **jug of water, please?**
¿puede traernos otra jarra de agua, por favor?
*pway-day tra-**air**-nos **oh**-tra **CHa-RRa** day **ag**-wa, por fa-**bor***

Understanding

¿han elegido ya?
are you ready to order?

vuelvo dentro de unos minutos
I'll come back in a few minutes

lo siento, no me queda/quedan…
I'm sorry, we don't have any… left

es una especie de...
it's a kind of...

¿qué quiere de tomar or **beber?**
what would you like to drink?

¿estaba todo bien?
was everything OK?

¿quiere postre o café?
would you like dessert or coffee?

BARS AND CAFÉS

Expressing yourself

what are you having?
¿qué vas a tomar?
*kay bas a toh-**mar***

I'd like…
quiero…
kyair-oh…

a Coke®/a diet Coke®
una Coca-Cola®/una Coca-Cola® light
oo-na koh-ka koh-la/oo-na koh-ka koh-la light

a glass of white/red wine
un vaso de vino blanco/tinto
*oon ba-soh day bee-noh blang-koh/
teen-toh*

a beer
una cerveza
oo-na sair-bay-sa

a draught beer
(Arg, Peru) una jarra *or* un chop, *(Carib)* una cerveza de barril, *(Mex)* un shot
oo-na CHa-RRa/oon shop/oo-na sair-bay-sa day ba-RReel/oon shot

a glass of water
un vaso de agua
oon ba-soh day ag-wa

a cup of tea
un té
oon tay

a black coffee/a coffee with milk
un café solo/con leche
oon ka-fay soh-loh/kon le-chay

a coffee and a croissant
un café y un croissant
oon ka-fay ee oon krwa-san

a hot chocolate
un chocolate
oon cho-koh-lah-tay

I'll have the same
para mí lo mismo
pa-ra mee loh mees-moh

the same again, please
lo mismo, por favor
loh meez-moh, por fa-bor

Understanding

sin alcohol
nonalcoholic

¿qué desea?
what would you like?

¿puede pagar ahora, por favor?
could I ask you to pay now, please?

ésta es la zona de no fumadores
this is the non-smoking area

Some informal expressions

estar borracho or *(Carib)* **ajumado** to be wasted
tener resaca or *(Mex)* **cruda,** *(Peru)* **estar resaqueado** to have a
hangover
estar borracho como una cuba or *(Carib)* **tuerca** to be as drunk as a
skunk

PAYING

Expressing yourself

the *(Am)* **check** or *(Br)* **bill, please**
la cuenta, por favor
la kwen-ta, por fa-bor

how much do I owe you?
¿cuánto le debo?
kwan-toh lay day-boh

do you take credit cards?
¿aceptan tarjetas de crédito?
a-sep-tan tar-CHay-tas day kred-ee-toh

I think there's a mistake *(Am)* **on the check** or *(Br)* **in the bill**
creo que hay un error en la cuenta
kray-oh kay eye oon e-RRor en la kwen-ta

is service included?
¿está incluido el servicio?
es-ta eeng-kloo-ee-doh el sair-bees-yoh

Understanding

¿van a pagar juntos?
are you all paying together?

el servicio (de mozos or *(Carib, Mex)* meseros or camareros) está
incluido
service is included

53

FOOD AND DRINK

Understanding

a caballo *(Arg)*	piece of roast or fried meat, topped with fried eggs
aderezado	dressed
ahumado	smoked
a la parrilla	grilled *(over charcoal or a wood fire)*
a la plancha	grilled *(on a hotplate or griddle)*
a la romana	deep-fried in batter
aliñado	dressed
a punto *(Arg)*	just right; medium *(steak)*
asado	roasted
asado en horno de leña	roasted in a wood-fired oven
braseado	braised
cocido	boiled
condimentado	dressed
curado	cured
dorado	browned
empanado	in breadcrumbs
en lonchas, *(Arg)* **en fetas,** *(Carib)* **en lascas,** *(Mex)* **en rebanadas,** *(Peru)* **en lonjas**	sliced
en puré	puréed
en su punto	just right; medium *(steak)*
en trozos	in pieces
estofado	stewed
fresco	fresh
frío	cold
frito	fried
fundido	melted
hecho	done, cooked
hervido	boiled
jugoso *(Arg)*	rare
montado *(Peru)*	piece of roast or fried meat, topped with fried eggs
poco hecho	rare

rebozado	battered; dipped in flour and egg
relleno	stuffed, filled
salteado	sautéed
término medio *(Carib, Peru)*	just right; medium *(steak)*

◆ desayunos y meriendas breakfasts and snacks

alfajor *(Arg)*	small cake filled with caramel, covered with chocolate or sugar
bizcochito *(Carib)*	small cake
bollo *(Mex)*	roll
churro	fritter *(often eaten dipped in thick chocolate)*
dona *(Carib, Mex, Peru)*	type of doughnut
factura *(Arg)*	small cake
magdalena	small sponge cake, madeleine
manteca *(Arg)*, **mantequilla**	butter
margarina	margarine
mermelada	jam
pancito *(Arg, Peru)*	roll
pan dulce *(Mex)*	small cake
panecillo *(Carib)*	roll
pastelito *(Peru)*	small cake
tostada	slice of toast

◆ aperitivos appetizers and savoury snacks

aceitunas	olives
alcapurrias *(Carib)*	fried plantain and cassava parcels stuffed with meat
anchoas	salted anchovies
bacalaítos *(Carib)*	fried cod pieces
berberechos	cockles
bonito en escabeche con pimientos	pickled tuna with roast peppers
boquerones en vinagre	pickled anchovies
boquerones fritos	(fresh) fried anchovies
calamares fritos	fried squid
camarones a la plancha	grilled prawns *or Am* shrimp
camarones cocidos	boiled prawns *or Am* shrimp

champiñones a la plancha	grilled mushrooms
chicharrones de pollo *(Peru)*	crispy deep-fried chicken skin
chicharrones de calamar *(Peru)*	crispy deep-fried squid
chorizo	spicy pork sausage
croquetas	croquettes
empanada gallega	pastry parcel filled with tuna or cod
empanadillas	savoury filled pastry parcels
ensalada rusa	Russian salad *(chopped mixed vegetables, cooked and served cold in a mayonnaise dressing)*
gordita *(Mex)*	corn tortilla filled with meat and spices
guacamole *(Mex)*	guacamole
langostinos cocidos	boiled prawns *or Am* shrimp
maníes	peanuts
mejillones al vapor	steamed mussels
mejillones en salsa	mussels in sauce
mollejas *(Arg)*	sweetbreads
morcilla *(Arg)*	blood sausage, *Br* ≈ black pudding
papas fritas	*Am* potato chips, *Br* crisps
pescadito frito	fried whitebait
pulpo a la gallega	boiled octopus dusted with hot paprika
salchichón	type of large, spicy, salami-like sausage
sandwich caliente *(Arg)*	toasted cheese and ham sandwich
tacos *(Mex)*	corn tortillas filled with meat and spices
tequeños *(Peru)*	small cheese sticks fried in dough
torta *(Mex)*	sandwich
tortilla española	potato omelette
tostadas *(Mex)*	crispy tortillas topped with refried beans, sour cream and salad
tostones *(Carib)*	fried sliced plantain
yuca frita *(Peru)*	cassava chips *or Br* crisps

♦ **primeros platos** first courses

acelgas	Swiss chard
alcachofas	artichokes
alitas de pollo *(Mex)*	chicken wings
alubias blancas	haricot beans
alubias rojas	red kidney beans

arroz con gandules *(Carib)*	rice with pigeon peas *(type of small pea)*
berenjenas rebozadas	fried *Am* eggplant *or Br* aubergines
calabacines rellenos	stuffed *Am* zucchini *or Br* courgettes
causa *(Peru)*	seasoned mashed potato layered with tuna, chicken or vegetables and served cold
cebiche *(Peru)*	fish marinated in lemon or lime juice
choritos a la chalaca *(Peru)*	shellfish with onion and lemon
consomé	consommé
crema de calabacín	cream of *Am* zucchini *or Br* courgette soup
deditos de queso *(Mex)*	deep-fried cheese fingers
ensalada de lechuga, tomate y cebolla	lettuce, tomato and onion salad
ensalada de pimientos rojos	red pepper salad
ensalada mixta	mixed salad
espaguetis	spaghetti
frejoles, frijoles	beans
habas	broad beans
huevos fritos	fried eggs
huevos rellenos	stuffed eggs *(usually filled with tuna)*
lentejas	lentils
macarrones	macaroni
menestra de verduras	mixed vegetables
mofongo *(Carib)*	fried plantain filled with chicken or seafood
nachos *(Mex)*	nachos, corn chips
ocopa *(Peru)*	potatoes in a creamy, spicy sauce with nuts
panucho *(Mex)*	soft corn tortilla filled with refried beans, chicken, tomatoes and avocado
papa a la huancaína *(Peru)*	potato with yellow pepper and cheese
pasteles *(Carib)*	balls of mashed plantain and cassava, filled with meat and boiled in a plantain leaf wrapping
pastelón de amarillo *(Carib)*	*Am* ground meat *or Br* mince with plantain

pozole *(Mex)*   stew with corn, pork and chili garnished with green leaves

quesadillas *(Mex)*   corn tortillas filled with cheese

solterito *(Peru)*   beans, corn and cheese

sopa de pescado   fish soup

sopes *(Mex)*   corn cakes with mashed beans and spiced ground beef/chicken/pork

taquitos fritos *(Mex)*   fried corn chips

tlacoyos *(Mex)*   corn cakes stuffed with refried beans, topped with onion and sour cream

tortilla de champiñones/ jamón y queso   mushroom/ham and cheese omelette

◆ **pescados** fish dishes

arroz con mariscos *(Peru)*   rice with seafood

atún encebollado   tuna with onion

bacalao   cod

boquerones   fresh anchovies

calamares a la plancha   grilled squid

calamares en su tinta   squid cooked in their ink

caldo de mariscos   shellfish broth

camarones a la diabla *(Mex)*   sautéed shrimp with spicy sauce

camarones fritos/adobados/ al mojo de ajo   fried/spicy/garlic shrimp

chaufa de mariscos *(Peru)*   Chinese-style fried rice with seafood

chipirones a la plancha   grilled baby squid

chipirones en su tinta   baby squid cooked in their ink

cóctel de camarones   shrimp cocktail

empanadas *(Peru)*   deep-fried pastry parcels filled with seafood

filete de pescado al mojo de ajo *(Mex)*   fish with garlic sauce

huachinango a la veracruzana *(Mex)*   red snapper fillet with sautéed tomatoes, onions, olives, capers and chillis

humita *(Arg)*   deep-fried pastry parcel filled with corn

jalea *(Peru)*   deep-fried pieces of fish and seafood

juey *(Carib)*	crab
lenguado a la plancha	grilled sole
merluza en salsa verde	hake in green sauce
merluza rebozada	hake in batter
mero	grouper
mojarra frita	fried whitebait
parihuela *(Peru)*	seafood stew
pescado a la menier *(Peru)*	fish fried in butter
pescado a lo macho *(Peru)*	fish in a seafood sauce
pez espada	swordfish
picante de mariscos *(Peru)*	seafood stew
pulpo	octopus
salmón a la parrilla	barbecued salmon
sardinas	sardines
sudado *(Peru)*	steamed fish with onions, tomatoes and potatoes
trucha con jamón	trout fried with ham

◆ aves y caza poultry and game

ají de gallina *(Peru)*	chicken in a spicy sauce with nuts
arroz chaufa *(Peru)*	Chinese-style fried rice
arroz con menudos	rice with chicken livers and hearts
arroz con pato/pollo *(Peru)*	rice with duck/chicken
codorniz escabechada	pickled quail
codorniz estofada	braised quail
conejo al ajillo	rabbit with garlic
enchiladas rojas de pollo *(Mex)*	corn tortillas stuffed with chicken in tomato sauce topped with cheese
enchiladas suizas *(Mex)*	corn tortillas stuffed with chicken in a creamy tomato sauce topped with cheese
escabeche de pollo	pickled chicken
estofado de pollo	chicken stew
jabalí	wild boar
milanesa de pollo *(Arg, Peru)*	chicken fillet fried in breadcrumbs
mole con pollo *(Mex)*	chicken topped with mole sauce (chili peppers and unsweetened chocolate) and sesame seeds

pato	duck
pechuga empanada	chicken breast fried in breadcrumbs
perdiz escabechada	pickled partridge
perdiz estofada	braised partridge
pollo a las brasas	barbecued chicken
pollo al ajillo	chicken with garlic
pollo asado	roast chicken
pollo en salsa de cacahuate y nuez *(Mex)*	chicken with peanut and walnut sauce
pollo en salsa verde *(Mex)*	chicken with salsa verde (green sauce made with a type of green tomato, herbs and spices)
seco de pollo *(Peru)*	stewed chicken with *Am* cilantro *or Br* coriander
suprema *(Arg, Peru)*	stuffed chicken fillet in breadcrumbs

◆ carnes meat dishes

albóndigas	meatballs
anticuchos *(Peru)*	kebabs made with beef hearts
arroz tapado *(Peru)*	rice with *Am* ground meat *or Br* mince, olives and sultanas
bife a la plancha *(Arg)*	grilled beef
bisctec a lo pobre *(Peru)*	veal fillet with fries, fried plantain and fried eggs
bistec apanado *(Peru)*	veal fillet in breadcrumbs
bistec encebollado *(Carib)*	beef with onion
carne asada	barbecued beef
carne estofada *or* guisada	meat stew
cordero asado	roast lamb
costilla de cerdo	pork chop
costillitas de cordero	lamb chops
costilla de ternera *or (Mex)* res	T-bone steak
empanada *(Carib)*	veal fillet in breadcrumbs
entrecot	entrecôte steak
escalope	escalope of veal
filete de cerdo	pork fillet
filete de ternera	veal fillet
lechazo asado	roast suckling lamb

lomo de cerdo asado	roast pork sirloin
lomo saltado *(Peru)*	sirloin steak sautéed with tomatoes, onions, potatoes and yellow pepper
milanesa *(Arg, Peru)*	veal fillet in breadcrumbs
pernil *(Carib)*	roast pork
rabo de buey	oxtail
solomillo	sirloin steak
ternera en su jugo	veal cooked in its own juices

◆ **postres y dulces** desserts and sweet things

arroz con leche	rice pudding
arroz zambito *(Peru)*	rice pudding with brown cane sugar
brazo gitano	type of sponge roll filled with cream
buñuelos	fritters
cajeta *(Mex)*	caramel made with goat's milk
casquitos de guayaba *(Carib)*	guava in syrup
cocada *(Mex)*	coconut with milk
coco amelcochao *(Carib)*	coconut *Am* candy *or Br* sweet
compota de manzana	stewed apple
crema catalana	type of crème brûlée
crepas de cajeta *(Mex)*	caramel crêpes
dulce de lechosa *(Carib)*	papaya in syrup
dulce de membrillo	quince jelly
duraznos en almíbar	peaches in syrup
flan	crème caramel
glorias *(Mex)*	caramels made with nuts
isla flotante *(Arg)*	soft meringue in a custard sauce
macedonia de frutas	fruit salad
mantecado	shortcake
manzana asada	baked apple
Martín Fierro *(Arg)*	cheese served with quince jelly
mazamorra morada *(Peru)*	purple corn
merengue	meringue
milhoja	puff pastry
mousse de lúcuma *(Peru)*	lucuma mousse *(popular Peruvian fruit)*
muégano *(Mex)*	caramel popcorn
natillas	custard
palanquetas *(Mex)*	caramel-coated peanuts

FOOD AND DRINK

pasta de guayaba *(Carib)*   guava paste
picarones *(Peru)*   sweet potato/squash with honey
suspiro a la limeña *(Peru)*   meringue with caramel
tembleque *(Carib)*   coconut crème caramel
tocino de cielo   dessert made with egg yolks and sugar

GLOSSARY OF FOOD AND DRINK

aceite oil
aceite de oliva olive oil
achicoria chicory
ácido sour, acidic
acompañante *(Carib)* accompaniment
agridulce sweet-and-sour
aguacate avocado
aguaje *(Peru)* buriti palm fruit
aguaymanto *(Peru)* cape gooseberry
ajo garlic
albahaca basil
alcachofa artichoke
alcaparras capers
alcaucil *(Arg)* artichoke
alioli garlic mayonnaise
almejas clams
almendras almonds
almíbar syrup
alubias beans
alubias negras black beans
alubias rojas red kidney beans
anchoas salted anchovies
angulas elvers
apio celery
arándano blackcurrant
arenque herring
arroz rice
arvejas *(Arg)* peas
asado roast, baked
asar to roast, to bake
atún tuna
avellana hazelnut
azafrán saffron
azúcar sugar
bacón bacon
bacalao cod
bacalao salado salt cod
banana banana
barbacoa barbecue

barra bar
barra de pan French loaf, baguette
batata *(Arg)* sweet potato
batido milkshake
bechamel béchamel sauce
berenjena *Am* eggplant, *Br* aubergine
berros watercress
besugo red sea-bream
biaaaho *(Carib)* relru
boquerones fresh anchovies
brócoli broccoli
brotes de soja bean sprouts
budín pudding
calabacín *Am* zucchini, *Br* courgette
calabaza pumpkin
calamar squid
caldo broth
calentar to heat (up)
camarones prawns, *Am* shrimp
camote *(Peru)* sweet potato
camu camu rum berry
canela cinnamon
canelones cannelloni
carne meat
carne picada *Am* ground meat, *Br* mince
castaña chestnut
cazón dogfish
cebolla onion
cebolleta type of large *Am* scallion *or Br*
     spring onion
centolla spider crab
cerdo pork
cerveza beer
chalote shallot
champiñones mushrooms
chayote *(Mex)* chayote squash
chícharos *(Mex)* peas
chilaca *(Mex)* cherry pepper (small hot, sweet
     pepper)

FOOD AND DRINK

chilacayote *(Mex)* chilacayote squash
chile serrano/poblano/jalapeño/ habanero/güero *(Mex)* chilli
chirimoya custard apple
choclo *(Arg, Peru)* corn
chocolate chocolate
chorizo spicy pork sausage
cilantro *Am* cilantro, *Br* coriander
ciruela plum
ciruela pasa, ciruela seca prune
clara de huevo egg white
clavo clove
cocinar to cook
coco coconut
cochinillo suckling pig
codorniz quail
cogollo lettuce heart, little gem lettuce
col cabbage
coles de Bruselas Brussels sprouts
coliflor cauliflower
comida food
comida chatarra junk food
comino cumin
complemento *(Carib)* accompaniment
conejo rabbit
congelado frozen
congrio conger eel
conservante preservative
conservar to preserve
coñac brandy
copos de avena oatflakes
copos de maíz tostados cornflakes
corazones de alcachofas artichoke hearts
cordero lamb
cortar to cut
costilla rib
crema batida whipped cream
crema *(Arg)* **doble** or *(Peru)* **de leche** *Am* heavy or *Br* double cream
crema pastelera confectioner's custard
crudo raw
crujiente crisp, crunchy
cuchara spoon
cucharada spoonful
cucharita, cucharilla teaspoon
deshuesado boned
derretido melted
diente de ajo clove of garlic
doble crema *(Mex)* *Am* heavy or *Br* double cream

dorada gilthead bream
dulce sweet
dulce de membrillo quince jelly
ejote *(Mex)* green bean
empanada savoury filled pastry
empanadilla small savoury filled pastry
en lata canned
endibias endives
endulzante sweetener
eneldo dill
entero whole
espaguetis spaghetti
espárragos asparagus
especias spices
espeso thick
espina (fish)bone
espinacas spinach
espuma foam, froth
fécula starch
filete fillet
freír to fry
fresa strawberry
fruta fruit
frutilla *(Arg)* strawberry
galleta cookie, *Br* biscuit
galleta salada cracker
garbanzos *Am* garbanzo beans, *Br* chickpeas
granada pomegranate
granos de pimienta peppercorns
grasa fat
gratinar to grill, to brown under the grill
guanábana *(Mex)* soursop *(type of tropical fruit)*
guarnición accompaniment *(to the main part of a dish)*
guayaba guava
guindilla hot pepper *(sometimes pickled)*
habas broad beans
harina flour
heladera *(Arg)* refrigerator
helado ice cream
hervir to boil
hierbabuena mint
hígado liver
higo fig
hinojo fennel
hojaldre puff pastry
hongos mushroom
horno oven
hueso bone

huevas roe
huevo egg
huevo duro hard-boiled egg
ingredientes ingredients
jabalí wild boar
jamón (cocido or *(Carib)* **de sandwich** or
  (Peru) **inglés)** boiled ham
jerez sherry
jícama *(Mex)* Mexican turnip
jitomate *(Mex)* tomato
langostinos prawns, *Am* shrimp
lata can
laurel bayleaf
leche milk
leche cuajada curd
lechuga lettuce
lenguado sole
lentejas lentils
liebre hare
lima lime
limón lemon
lomo *(Arg)* fillet
lúcuma lucuma *(type of Peruvian fruit)*
maduro mature, ripe
maíz (sweet)corn
malanga *(Carib)* taro *(type of root vegetable)*
mango mango
manteca lard, *(Arg)* butter
mantequilla butter
manzana apple
maracuyá passion fruit
margarina margarine
mariscos seafood
masitas cakes
mayonesa mayonnaise
mejillones mussels
melocotón peach
melón melon
membrillo quince
menta mint
merluza hake
miel honey
mora blackberry
morcilla blood sausage, *Br* black pudding
mostaza mustard
muslo de pollo chicken drumstick
naranja orange
nectarina nectarine
nopal *(Mex)* prickly pear
nueces walnuts

nuez moscada nutmeg
ñame *(Carib)* yam
orégano oregano
palta *(Arg, Peru)* avocado
pan bread
pan de molde sliced bread
pan flauta *(Arg)* French loaf, baguette
pan integral wholewheat or *Br* wholemeal
  bread
pan rallado breadcrumbs
pana *(Carib)* breadfruit
panceta bacon
pancho *(Arg)* hotdog
papa potato
papas fritas *Am* potato chips, *Br* crisps
papalo *(Mex)* type of Mexican cooking herb
papaya papaya
parrillada *(Arg)* grill; barbecue
pasa currant
pasta pasta
pastel cake
pato duck
pechuga de pollo chicken breast
pepino cucumber
pera pear
perdiz partridge
perejil parsley
pescado fish
pez espada swordfish
picante hot, spicy
pimentón paprika
pimienta pepper
pimiento rojo red pepper
pimiento verde green pepper
piña pineapple
piñones pine nuts
plátano banana
plato dish; course; plate
plato combinado meal served together on
  one plate, instead of as separate dishes
pollo chicken
pomelo grapefruit
postre dessert
pulpo octopus
puerros leeks
quenepa *(Carib)* honeyberry *(fruit similar to
  a blueberry)*
queque *(Peru)* cake
queso cheese
rabanito radish

receta recipe
refresco soft drink
refrigerador, refrigeradora refrigerator
remolacha *Am* beet, *Br* beetroot
riñones kidneys
romero rosemary
sabor taste, flavour
sal salt
salado salted; salty
salchicha sausage, *(Peru)* hot dog
salmón salmon
salmonete red mullet
salsa sauce
sandía watermelon
sarandaja *(Peru)* type of bean
sardinas sardines
sartén frying pan
semillas seeds
sidra *Am* hard cider, *Br* cider
sofrito fried tomato, onion and garlic
solomillo sirloin
tallarines tagliarini *(type of pasta)*

tarta de queso cheesecake
tarwi *(Peru)* tarwi *(bean from a type of Andean lupin plant)*
ternera veal
tierno tender
tocino bacon
tomate tomato
tomillo thyme
torrija French toast
torta *(Arg)* cake
tortilla (de papas) potato omelette
tostada slice of toast
trucha trout
verdolaga purslane *(green leafy vegetable)*
vinagre vinegar
vino wine
yautía *(Carib)* tania fruit
yema de huevo egg yolk
yemas *Am* candies *or Br* sweets made with egg yolks and sugar
yuca *(Carib)* cassava
zanahoria carrot

GOING OUT

(i)

Latin America has a vibrant nightlife. Going out for **el fin de semana** (the weekend) is a ritual, but even on Thursdays there are plenty of people out and about. On Fridays and Saturdays the streets are almost invariably thronged with people, who go out late – generally from about 10 or 11 p.m., often staying out until dawn. You can find plenty of information about what's going on in magazines like **Guía del Ocio** or **Tiempo Libre** (out every Thursday), which have information on shows, concerts, nightclubs and so on. You can also consult the local newspapers.

Going to the cinema is cheaper than at home, but note that foreign-language films are sometimes dubbed into Spanish. Films that are not dubbed are labelled versión original subtitulada, often abbreviated to V.O.S. (original version with subtitles).

Latin American nightclubs are generally open until the small hours (between 3 and 5 a.m.). The minimum age for admittance is 18.

The basics

ballet	ballet *ba-let*
band	grupo *groo-poh*
bar	bar *bar*
book	libro *lee-broh*
cinema *(Br)*	cine *see-nay*
circus	circo *seer-koh*
classical music	música clásica *moo-see-ka kla-see-ka*
club	discoteca *dees-koh-tay-ka*
concert	concierto *kon-syair-toh*
dubbed film	película doblada *pe-lee-koo-la doh-blah-da*
festival	festival *fes-tee-bal*
film	película *pe-lee-koo-la*
folk music	música popular *moo-see-ka pop-oo-lar*
group	grupo *groo-poh*
jazz	jazz *yaz*
modern dance	danza moderna *dan-sa mod-air-na*

movie	película *pe-**lee**-koo-la*
movie theater *(Am)*	cine *see-nay*
musical	musical *moo-see-**kahl***
party	fiesta *fyes-ta*
pop music	música pop *moo-see-ka pop*
rock music	música rock *moo-see-ka rok*
show	espectáculo *es-pek-**tak**-oo-loh*
subtitled film	película subtitulada *pe-**lee**-koo-la soob-tee-too-**lah**-da*
theater/theatre	teatro *tay-**ah**-troh*
ticket	entrada *en-**trah**-da*
to go out	salir *sa-**leer***
to play *(music)*	poner *pon-**air***

SUGGESTIONS AND INVITATIONS

Expressing yourself

where can we go?
¿dónde podemos ir?
*don-day pod-**ay**-mos eer*

what do you want to do?
¿qué quieres hacer?
*kay **kyair**-es a-**sair***

shall we go for a drink?
¿vamos a tomar una copa *or* un trago *or (Arg, Carib)* algo?
*bah-mos a toh-**mar** oo-na **koh**-pa/oon tra-goh/**al**-goh*

what are you doing tonight?
¿qué haces esta noche?
*kay **a**-ses **es**-ta **no**-chay*

do you have plans?
¿tienes planes?
*tyen-es **plah**-nays*

would you like to…?
¿te gustaría…?, ¿quieres…?
*tay goos-ta-**ree**-a…/**kyair**-es…*

we were thinking of going to…
estábamos pensando en ir a…
*es-**tah**-ba-mos pen-**san**-doh en eer a…*

I'd love to
me encantaría
*may eng-kan-ta-**ree**-a*

I'm not sure I can make it
creo que no puedo
*kray-oh kay noh **pway**-doh*

I can't today, but maybe some other time
hoy no puedo, pero quizás otro día
*oy noh **pway**-doh, **pe**-roh kee-**sas** oh-troh **dee**-a*

ARRANGING TO MEET

Expressing yourself

what time shall we meet?
¿a qué hora quedamos or nos encontramos?
*a kay **aw**-ra kay-**dah**-mos/nos eng-kon-**trah**-mos*

where shall we meet?
¿dónde quedamos or nos encontramos?
*don-day kay-**dah**-mos/nos eng-kon-**trah**-mos*

would it be possible to meet a bit later?
¿podemos quedar or encontrarnos un poco más tarde?
*pod-**ay**-mos kay-**dar**/en-kon-**trar**-nos oon **poh**-koh mas **tar**-day*

I have to meet… at nine
he quedado or me voy a encontrar con… a las nueve
*ay kay-**dah**-doh/may boy a eng-kon-**trar** kon… a las **nway**-bay*

I don't know where it is, but I'll find it on the map
no sé dónde está, pero lo encontraré en el mapa
*no say **don**-day es-**ta**, **pe**-roh loh eng-kon-trah-**ray** en el **ma**-pa*

I'll meet you later, I have to stop by the hotel first
nos vemos luego, tengo que pasar por el hotel primero
*nos **bay**-mos **lway**-goh, **teng**-goh kay pa-**sar** por el oh-**tel** pree-**mair**-oh*

I'll call/text you if there's a change of plan
te llamo/mando un mensaje si hay cambio de planes
*tay **yah**-moh/**man**-doh oon men-**sa**-CHay see hay **kam**-byoh day **plah**-nays*

sorry I'm late
siento llegar tarde
*syen-toh yay-**gar** **tar**-day*

see you tomorrow night
nos vemos mañana
*nos **bay**-mos man-**yah**-na*

Understanding

¿te parece bien?
is that ok with you?

nos vemos allí
I'll meet you there

pasaré a recogerte sobre las ocho
I'll come and pick you up about 8

podemos quedar or **encontrarnos afuera...**
we can meet outside...

te voy a dar mi número y puedes llamarme mañana
I'll give you my number and you can call me tomorrow

Some informal expressions

tomar una copa or **un trago** or *(Arg, Carib)* **algo** to have a drink
picar algo to have a bite to eat
pasarlo en grande or *(Carib)* **gozar** to have a blast

MOVIES, SHOWS AND CONCERTS

Expressing yourself

is there a guide to *(Am)* **what's playing** or *(Br)* **what's on?**
¿hay una Guía del ocio or *(Mex)* revista Tiempo libre?
*eye oo-na **gee**-a del os-yoh/ray-**bees**-ta **tyem**-po **lee**-bray*

two tickets, please
dos entradas, por favor
*dos en-**trah**-das, por fa-**bor***

I'd like three tickets for...
quiero tres entradas para...
*kyair-oh trays en-**trah**-das pa-ra...*

it's called...
se llama...
*say **yah**-ma...*

what time does it start?
¿a qué hora empieza?
*a kay **aw**-ra em-**pyay**-sa*

I've seen the trailer
he visto el tráiler or la sinopsis
*ay **bees**-toh el **treye**-lair/la see-**nop**-sees*

I'd like to go and see a show
me gustaría ir a ver un espectáculo
*may goos-ta-**ree**-a eer a bair oon es-pek-**tak**-oo-loh*

I'll find out whether there are still tickets available
voy a ver si todavía quedan entradas
*boy a bair see toh-da-**bee**-a **kay**-dan en-**trah**-das*

do we need to book in advance?
¿hay que reservar con antelación?
*eye kay res-air-**bar** kon an-tay-las-**yohn***

how long will it be *(Am)* **playing** *or (Br)* **on for?**
¿cuánto dura?
***kwan**-toh **doo**-ra*

are there tickets for another day?
¿hay entradas para otro día?
*eye en-**trah**-das **pa**-ra **oh**-troh **dee**-a*

I'd like to go to a bar with some live music
me gustaría ir a un bar con música en vivo
*may goos-ta-**ree**-a eer a oon bar con **moo**-see-ka en **bee**-boh*

are there any free concerts?
¿hay conciertos gratis?
*eye kon-**syair**-tohs **grah**-tees*

what sort of music is it?
¿qué tipo de música es?
*kay **tee**-poh day **moo**-see-ka es*

Understanding

boletería	box office
cine de arte y ensayo	arthouse *(Am)* movie theater *or (Br)* cinema
matiné	matinée
reservas	bookings

estreno en cines el...
on general release from...

la estrenan la semana que viene
it comes out next week

ha tenido muy buenas críticas
it's had very good reviews

es un concierto al aire libre
it's an open-air concert

la dan *or* **pasan en el Odeón a las ocho**
it's *(Am)* playing *or (Br)* on at 8 p.m. at the Odeón

esa sesión *or (Carib)* **tanda está agotada**
that showing's sold out

está todo agotado *or (Carib)* **vendido hasta…**
it's all booked up until…

no hace falta reservar con antelación
there's no need to book in advance

se recomienda llegar un cuarto de hora antes
you should arrive quarter of an hour before it starts

la obra dura dos horas con el entreacto
the play lasts two hours, including the *(Am)* intermission *or (Br)* interval

por favor apaguen sus teléfonos celulares
please turn off your *(Am)* cellphones *or (Br)* mobile phones

PARTIES AND CLUBS

Expressing yourself

I'm having *(Am)* **a going-away party** *or (Br)* **a leaving party tonight**
voy a hacer una fiesta de despedida esta noche
boy a a-sair oo-na fyes-ta day des-pe-dee-da es-ta no-CHay

should I bring something to drink?
¿llevo algo de tomar?
yay-boh al-goh day toh-mar

we could go to a club after that
podemos ir a una discoteca luego
po-day-mos eer a oo-na dees-koh-tay-ka lway-goh

do you have to pay to get in?
¿hay que pagar entrada?
eye kay pa-gar en-trah-da

I have to meet someone inside
he quedado *or* me voy a encontrar con alguien adentro
ay kay-dah-doh/may boy a eng-kon-trar kon al-gyen a-den-troh

will you let me back in when I come back?
¿me dejarás entrar cuando vuelva?
may day-CHa-ras en-trar kwan-doh bwel-ba

the DJ's really cool
el disk-jockey es genial
el dees-yok-ey es CHen-yahl

do you come here often?
¿vienes mucho por aquí?
byen-es moo-choh por a-kee

can I buy you a drink?
¿te puedo invitar un trago?
tay pway-doh een-bee-tar oon trah-goh

no thanks, I don't smoke
no gracias, no fumo
noh gras-yas, noh foo-moh

thanks, but I'm with my boyfriend
gracias, pero estoy con mi novio
gras-yas, pe-roh es-toy kon mee noh-boh

Understanding

consumisión gratis	free drink
guardarropa	*(Am)* coat check, *(Br)* cloakroom
70 pesos depúes de las 12	70 pesos after midnight

hay una fiesta en casa de Elena
there's a party at Elena's place

eres muy guapo/a, *(Arg)* **sos muy lindo/a,** *(Carib)* **estás bueno/a**
you're very attractive

¿quieres bailar?
do you want to dance?

¿quieres algo de beber?
would you like a drink?

¿tienes fuego?
do you have a light?

¿tienes un cigarrillo?
do you have a cigarette?

¿quedamos para *or* **podemos vernos otro día?**
can we see each other again?

¿puedo acompañarte a casa?
can I see you home?

TOURISM AND SIGHTSEEING

Museums in Latin America are generally open Tuesday to Sunday from 10 a.m. to 5 p.m. Most museums, as well as many monuments and churches, charge an admission fee (though some are free to locals). Student discounts are available. Opening hours may change according to the season.

The basics

ancient	antiguo *an-**tee**-gwoh*
antique *(noun)*	antigüedad *an-tee-gway-dad*
area	zona *soh-na*
castle	castillo *kas-**tee**-yoh*
cathedral	catedral *ka-tay-**drahl***
century	siglo *see-gloh*
church	iglesia *ee-**glay**-sya*
city centre, *(Am)* **downtown**	centro (de la ciudad) *sen-troh (day la syoo-dad)*
exhibition, *(Am)* **exhibit**	exposición *eks-poh-sees-**yohn***
fort	fuerte *fwair-tay*
gallery	galería *ga-lair-**ee**-a*
modern art	arte moderno *ar-tay mo-**dair**-noh*
mosque	mezquita *mes-**kee**-ta*
museum	museo *moo-**say**-oh*
painting	*(art)* pintura *peen-**too**-ra*; *(picture)* cuadro *kwad-roh*
park	parque *par-kay*
pyramid	pirámide *pee-**ra**-mee-day*
ruins	ruinas *rwee-nas*
sculpture	escultura *es-kool-**too**-ra*
statue	estatua *es-**tat**-wa*
street map	plano *plah-noh*
synagogue	sinagoga *see-na-**goh**-ga*
tour guide	guía turistico *gee-a too-**rees**-tee-ko*

tourist	turista *too-rees-ta*
tourist information centre, tourist office	oficina de información turística *o-fee-see-na day een-for-mas-yohn too-rees-tee-ka*

Expressing yourself

I'd like some information on…
quisiera información sobre…
kees-yair-a een-for-mas-yohn soh-bray…

can you tell me where the tourist office is?
¿puede decirme dónde está la oficina de información turística?
pway-day de-seer-may don-day es-ta la o-fee-see-na day een-for-mas-yhon too-rees-tee-ka

do you have a street map of the town?
¿tiene un plano de la ciudad?
tyen-ay oon plah-noh day la syoo-dad

I was told there's a museum around here
me han dicho que hay un museo por aquí
may an dee-choh kay eye oon moo-say-oh por a-kee

can you show me where it is on the map?
¿me lo puede señalar en el mapa?
may loh pway-day sen-ya-lar en el ma-pa

how do you get there?
¿cómo se llega allí?
koh-oh say yay-ga a-yee

when was it built?
¿cuándo fue construido?
kwan-doh fway kons-troo-ee-doh

is it free?
¿es gratis?
es grah-tees

is there disabled access?
¿hay acceso para minusválidos?
eye ak-say-soh pa-ra mee-noos-bal-ee-dohs

Understanding

abierto	open
casco antiguo	old town
cerrado	closed

ciudad vieja	old town
criollo	Latin American with European origin
entrada gratuita	admission free
guerra	war
indígena	indigenous
invasión	invasion
precolombino	pre-Columbian
renovación	renovation
trabajos de restauración	restoration work
usted está aquí	you are here *(on a map)*
visita guiada	guided tour

pregunte cuando llegue allí
you'll have to ask when you get there

la proxima visita guiada empieza a las dos
the next guided tour starts at 2 o'clock

MUSEUMS, GALLERIES AND MONUMENTS

Expressing yourself

I've heard there's a... *(Am)* **exhibit** or *(Br)* **exhibition on at the moment**
he oído que hay una exposición de… ahora
ay o-ee-doh kay eye oo-na eks-poh-sees-yohn day... a-aw-ra

how much is it to get in?
¿cuánto es la entrada?
kwan-toh es la en-trah-da

is it open on Sundays?
¿está abierto los domingos?
es-ta ab-yair-toh los do-meen-gohs

is this ticket valid for the *(Am)* **exhibit** or *(Br)* **exhibition as well?**
¿esta entrada también es válida para la exposición?
es-ta en-trah-da tam-byen es bal-ee-da pa-ra la eks-poh-sees-yohn

are there any student discounts?
¿hay descuentos para estudiantes?
eye des-kwen-tohs pa-ra es-tood-yan-tays

TOURISM, SIGHTSEEING

75

one full ticket and two *(Am)* **discounts** *or (Br)* **concessions, please**
por favor, una entrada normal y dos con descuento
por fa-bor, oo-na en-trah-da nor-mahl ee dos kon des-kwen-toh

how long does the visit take?
¿cuánto dura la visita?
kwan-toh doo-ra la bee-see-ta

I have a student card
tengo carnet de estudiante
teng-goh kar-nay day es-tood-yan-tay

Understanding

audioguía	audioguide
boletería	ticket office
exposición permanente/ temporal	permanent/temporary *(Am)* exhibit *or (Br)* exhibition
prohibido sacar *or* tomar fotos	no photography
prohibido usar el flash	no flash photography
se ruega no tocar	please do not touch
silencio, por favor	silence, please

la entrada al museo cuesta…
admission to the museum costs…

con esta entrada también puede entrar a la exposición
this ticket also allows you access to the *(Am)* exhibit *or (Br)* exhibition

¿tienes el carnet de estudiante?
do you have your student card *or* student ID?

hay una visita guiada en inglés que empieza dentro de cinco minutos
there's a guided tour in English starting in five minutes

GIVING YOUR IMPRESSIONS

Expressing yourself

it's beautiful
es precioso
es pres-yoh-soh

it's fantastic
es fantástico
es fan-tas-tee-koh

I really enjoyed it
me ha gustado mucho
may ha goos-tah-doh moo-choh

I didn't like it that much
no me ha gustado mucho
noh may ha goos-tah-doh moo-choh

I'm not really a fan of modern art
no me interesa mucho el arte moderno
noh may een-tay-ray-sa moo-choh el ar-tay mo-dair-noh

it's expensive for what it is
es caro para lo que es
es ka-roh pa-ra loh kay es

it was a bit boring
fue un poco aburrido
fway oon poh-koh a-boo-RRee-doh

it's very touristy
es muy turistico
es mwee too-rees-tee-koh

it was really crowded
había mucha gente
a-bee-a moo-cha CHen-tay

we didn't go in the end, the *(Am)* **line** *or (Br)* **queue was too long**
al final no entramos, la cola era demasiado larga
al fee-nal noh en-trah-mos, la koh-la air-a day-mas-yah-doh lar-ga

we didn't have time to see everything
no tuvimos tiempo de ver todo
noh too-bee-mos tyem-poh day bair toh-doh

Understanding

famoso	famous
pintoresco	picturesque
típico	typical
tradicional	traditional

no dejen de ir a ver…
you must go and see…

les recomiendo ir a…
I recommend going to…

hay una vista preciosa de toda la ciudad
there's a wonderful view over the whole city

se ha vuelto demasiado turístico
it's become a bit too touristy

SPORTS AND GAMES

Latin America offers plenty of opportunities for adventure and eco-tourism, as well as outdoor sports including hiking, mountain climbing, canyoning, diving, rafting and caving. The best areas for such activities include Veracruz, Zacatecas, Chihuahua, Mexico, Morelos, San Luis Potosí, Quintana Roo and Durango in Mexico, as well as Patagonia in Argentina and Cuzco in Peru. Skiing is possible in Bariloche (Argentina). Options for eco-tourism and rural tourism range from staying on an Argentinian ranch (**estancia**) to workshops on traditional medicine and spiritual retreats in Oaxaca, Michoacan or Yucatan (Mexico). The Mexican Caribbean is excellent for scuba diving. Hikers will find information and maps in tourist offices (**oficinas de turismo**) and equipment rental shops. Football is very popular and passions run high over certain matches; information on these can be found in local newspapers.

The basics

ball	pelota *pay-loh-ta*, *(Carib)* bola *boh-la*
basketball	básquet(bol) *bas-ket(-bol)*, *(Carib)* baloncesto *ba-lon-ses-to*
bike	bicicleta *bee-see-klay-ta*
board game	juego de mesa *CHway-goh day may-sa*
cards	cartas *kar-tas*
chess	ajedrez *a-CHay-dres*
cycling	ciclismo *see-klees-moh*
foosball *(Am)*	futbolito *foot-bol-ee-toh*, *(Peru)* fulbito de mano *fool-bee-toh day mah-noh*
football	*(Am) (American football)* fútbol americano *foot-bol a-mair-ee-kah-noh*; *(Br) (soccer)* fútbol *foot-bol*
game *(of football, basketball)*	partido *par-tee-doh*, *(Carib)* juego *CHway-goh*
hiking path	sendero *sen-dair-oh*
match	partido *par-tee-doh*, *(Carib)* juego *CHway-goh*
mountain biking	ciclismo de montaña *see-klees-moh day mon-tan-ya*

pool *(game)*	billar (americano) *beel-yar (a-mair-ee-kah-noh)*
rugby	rugby *roog-bee*
skiing	esquí *es-kee*
soccer	fútbol *foot-bol*
sport	deporte *day-por-tay*
surfing	surfing *soor-feeng*
swimming	natación *na-tas-yohn*
swimming pool	piscina *pee-see-na*, (Mex) alberca *al-bair-ka*
table football *(Br)*	futbolito *foot-bol-ee-toh*, (Peru) fulbito de mano *fool-bee-toh day mah-noh*
tennis	tenis *ten-ees*
waterskiing	esquí acuático *es-kee a kwat-ee-koh*
to go hiking	(Arg, Carib, Peru) hacer caminatas *a-sair ka-mee-na-tas*, (Mex) hacer senderismo *a-sair son dair-ees-moh*
to play...	jugar a... *CHoo-gar a...*
to ski	esquiar *es-kee-ar*

Expressing yourself

are there... lessons available?
¿dan clases de...?
dan kla-says day...

I'd like to rent... for an hour
quiero alquilar... por una hora
kyair-oh al-kee-lar ... por oo-na aw-ra

how much is it per person per hour?
¿cuánto es la hora por persona?
kwan-toh es la aw-ra por pair-soh-na

I'm not very athletic
no soy muy deportista
noh soy mwee day-por-tees-ta

I've never done it before
nunca lo he hecho
noong-ka loh ay ech-oh

I've done it once or twice, a long time ago
lo hice una o dos veces hace mucho tiempo
loh ee-say oo-na oh dos bes-ays a-say moo-choh tyem-poh

I'd like to go and watch *(Am)* **a soccer game** *or (Br)* **a football match**
me gustaría ir a ver un partido *or (Carib)* juego de fútbol
may goos-ta-ree-a eer a bair oon par-tee-doh/CHway-goh day foot-bol

let's stop for a picnic	**I'm exhausted!**
paremos a comer algo	¡estoy agotado!
*pa-**ray**-mos a kom-**air** al-goh*	*es-**toy** a-goh-**tah**-doh*

Understanding

alquiler de… ...for rent

¿tienes experiencia o eres principiante?
do you have any experience, or are you a complete beginner?

hay una garantía *or (Carib)* **un depósito de…**
there is a deposit of…

el seguro es obligatorio y cuesta…
insurance is compulsory and costs…

HIKING

Expressing yourself

can you go hiking around here?
¿se puede hacer *(Arg, Carib, Peru)* caminatas *or (Mex)* senderismo por
  aquí?
*say **pway**-day a-**sair** ka-mee-**na**-tas/sen-dair-**ees**-moh por a-**kee***

can you recommend any good walks in the area?
¿puede recomendarme algunas buenas rutas por esta zona?
***pway**-day re-kom-en-**dar**-may alg-**oo**-nas **bway**-nas **roo**-tas por la **soh**-na*

we're looking for a short walk somewhere around here
queremos dar un pequeño paseo por aquí
*kair-**ay**-mos dar oon pay-**ken**-yoh pa-**say**-oh por a-**kee***

can I rent hiking boots?
¿alquilan botines *or* botas de senderismo?
*al-**kee**-lan boh-**tee**-nays/**boh**-tas day sen-dair-**ees**-moh*

they don't fit	**is it very steep?**
no me quedan bien	¿es muy empinado?
*noh may **kay**-dan byen*	*es mwee em-pee-**nah**-doh*

how long does the walk take?
¿cuánto dura el recorrido?
kwan-toh doo-ra el ray-ko-RRee-doh

where's the start of the path?
¿dónde empieza el sendero?
don-day em-pyay-sa el sen-dair-oh

is the path marked *or* **signposted?**
¿está señalizado el sendero?
es-ta sen-ya-lee-sah-doh el sen-dair-oh

is it a circular path?
¿el sendero da una vuelta completa?
el sen-dair-oh dah oo-na bwel-ta com-play-ta

Understanding

duración media   average duration *(of walk)*

el recorrido dura unas tres horas, contando los descansos
it's about three hours' walk, including rest stops

traiga chaqueta impermeable y calzado *(Arg, Carib, Peru)* **para
caminata** *or (Mex)* **de senderismo**
bring a waterproof jacket and some walking shoes

OTHER SPORTS

Expressing yourself

where can we rent bikes?
¿dónde podemos alquilar bicicletas?
don-day pod-ay-mos al-kee-lar bee-see-klay-tas

are there any *(Am)* **bike paths** *or (Br)* **cycle paths?**
¿hay *(Arg, Peru)* ciclovías *or (Mex)* rutas ciclistas?
eye see-klo-bee-as/roo-tas see-klees-tas

I'd like to rent some climbing equipment
quisiera alquilar un equipo de escalar
kees-yair-a al-kee-lar oon ay-kee-poh day es-ka-lar

I've been climbing before
ya he escalado otras veces
yah ay es-ka-lah-doh oh-tras bay-says

does anyone have (Am) **a soccer ball** or (Br) **a football?**
¿alguien tiene una pelota or (Carib) bola?
al-gyen tyen-ay oo-na pay-loh-ta/boh-la

which team do you support?
¿de qué equipo eres?
day kay ay-kee-poh ay-res

I support...
yo soy de...
yoh soy day...

I run for half an hour every morning
corro media hora todas las mañanas
koRR-oh med-ya aw-ra toh-das las man-yah-nas

is there an open-air swimming pool?
¿hay piscina or (Mex) alberca al aire libre?
eye pee-see-na/al-bair-ka al eye-ray lee-bray

I've never been diving before
nunca he hecho buceo
noong-ka ay ech-oh boo-say-oh

I'd like to take beginners' sailing lessons
quiero tomar or (Carib) coger clases de vela para principiantes
kyair-oh toh-mar/ko-CHair klas-ays day bay-la pa-ra preen-see-pyan-tays

what do I do if the kayak capsizes?
¿qué hago si el kayak se vuelca?
kay ah-goh see el ka-yak say bwel-ka

Understanding

hay una cancha de tenis en el club cerca de la estación
there's a tennis court in the club near the station

la cancha de tenis está ocupada
the tennis court's occupied

¿es la primera vez que anda or **monta a caballo** or *(Carib)* **corre caballo?**
is this the first time you've been *(Am)* horseback riding or *(Br)* horse-riding?

¿sabe nadar?
can you swim?

INDOOR GAMES

Expressing yourself

how about a game of cards/Monopoly?®
¿jugamos una partida or un partido de cartas/Monopoly®?
CHoo-ga-mos oo-na par-tee dah/oon par-tee-doh day kar-tas/mo-noh-pohl-ee

does anyone know any good card games?
¿alguien sabe un buen juego de cartas?
al-gyen sah-bay oon bwen CHway-goh day kar-tas

it's your turn
te toca
tay toh-ka

Understanding

¿sabes jugar al ajedrez?
do you know how to play chess?

¿tienes una baraja de cartas?
do you have a pack of cards?

Some informal expressions

estoy muerto/a or **desbarato/a** or **hecho/a polvo** I'm exhausted
me ha machacado he totally thrashed me

SHOPPING

Shops in Latin America are generally open weekdays from 9 a.m. to 8.30 p.m. and Saturdays from 9 a.m. to 1 p.m., though hours can vary depending on the area. In tourist areas, opening hours vary according to the season, and many shops are open on Sundays in high season. Hypermarkets and shopping centres are usually open from 10 a.m. to 10 p.m. Big cities like Buenos Aires, Lima and Mexico City have 24-hour supermarkets. Cigarettes are relatively cheap and are sold at grocers' (*Arg* **almacenes**, *Peru* **bodegas**), service stations and markets. There are no vending machines in Latin America. If you pay for purchases by credit or debit card, you will be given the receipt to sign and will always be asked for ID.

Traditional markets play a key role in Mexican and Peruvian life, despite stiff competition from supermarkets. Most markets are open every day except Sunday, traditionally only in the morning, although some reopen in the afternoon. Markets are a good place to buy local handicrafts.

You can buy items including water, tissues, chewing gum and socks from street vendors.

The basics

bakery	panadería *pan-a-dair-ee-a*
butcher's	carnicería *kar-nee-sair-ee-a*
cash desk *(Br)*	caja *ka-CHa*
cheap	barato *ba-rah-toh*
checkout	caja *ka-CHa*
clothes	ropa *roh-pa*
department store	grandes tiendas *gran-days tyen-das*
expensive	caro *ka-roh*
grams	gramos *grah-mohs*
greengrocer's	verdulería *bair-doo-lair-ee-a*
grocer's, *(Am)* grocery store	tienda de comestibles, *(Arg)* almacén *tyen-da day kom-es-tee-blays/al-ma-sayn*
hypermarket	hipermercado *ee-pair-mair-kah-doh*

kilo	kilo *kee*-loh
mall *(Am)*	centro comercial *sen*-troh kom-air-*syal*, *(Arg)* shopping *shop*-eeng
present	regalo ray-*gah*-loh
price	precio *pres*-yoh
receipt	recibo ray-*see*-boh
refund *(noun)*	devolución day-bol-oos-*yohn*
register(s) *(Am)*	caja ka-*CHa*
sales	ofertas o-*fair*-tas, liquidación lee-kee-das-*yohn*, *(Carib)* especiales es-pay-*syah*-lays
sales assistant	vendedor ben-day-*dor*, *(Carib)* empleado em-*play-uh*-doh
shop	tienda *tyen*-da
shopping centre *(Br)*	centro comercial *sen*-troh kom-air-*syahl*, *(Arg)* shopping *shop*-eeng
souvenir	recuerdo ray-*kwair*-doh
store *(Am)*	tienda *tyen*-da
supermarket	supermercado soo-pair-mair-*kah*-doh
to buy	comprar kom-*prar*
to cost	costar kos-*tar*
to pay	pagar pa-*gar*
to sell	vender ben-*dair*
to refund	devolver day-bol-*bair*

SHOPPING

Expressing yourself

is there a supermarket near here?
¿hay un supermercado cerca?
eye oon soo-pair-mair-kah-doh sair-ka

where can I buy cigarettes?
¿dónde puedo comprar cigarrillos?
don-day pway-doh kom-prar see-ga-RRee-yohs

I'd like...
quiero...
kyair-oh...

do you sell...?
¿venden...?
ben-den...

do you know where I might find some…?
¿sabe dónde puedo encontrar…?
sab-ay don-day pway-doh eng-kon-trar…

can you order it for me?
¿me lo puede encargar *or* conseguir?
may loh pway-day en-kar-gar/kon-say-geer

how much is this?
¿cuánto es esto?
kwan-toh es es-toh

I don't have much money
no tengo mucho dinero
noh teng-goh moo-choh dee-nair-oh

I don't have enough money
no tengo suficiente dinero
noh teng-goh soo-fee-syen-tay dee-nair-oh

I'll take it
me lo llevo
may loh yay-boh

that's everything, thanks
eso es todo, gracias
es-oh es toh-doh, gras-yas

can I have a (plastic) bag?
¿me da una bolsa (de plástico)?
may dah oo-na bol-sa (day plas-tee-koh)

I think you've made a mistake with my change
creo que me ha dado mal el vuelto *or* cambio
kray-oh kay may a dah-doh mal el bwel-toh/kam-hynh

Understanding

abierto de… a…	open from… to…
cerrado los domingos/de	closed Sundays/1 p.m. to 3 p.m.
1 a 3 de la tarde	
especiales *(Carib)*	sales
liquidación	sales
oferta especial	special offer
ofertas	sales

¿quiere alguna cosa más?
will there be anything else?

¿quiere una bolsa?
would you like a bag?

PAYING

where do I pay?
¿dónde se paga?
don-day say pa-ga

how much do I owe you?
¿cuánto le debo?
kwan-toh lay day-boh

could you write it down for me, please?
¿me lo puede escribir, por favor?
may loh pway-day es-kree-heer por fa-bor

can I pay by credit card?
¿puedo pagar con tarjeta de crédito?
pway-doh pa-gar kon tar-CHay-tah day kred-ee-toh

I'll pay in cash
voy a pagar en efectivo
boy a pa-gar en ef-ek-tee-boh

can I have a receipt?
¿me da un recibo?
may da oon ray-see-boh

I'm sorry, I don't have any change
lo siento, no tengo cambio
loh syen-toh, noh teng-goh kam-byoh

can you give me change for a 500-peso *(Am)* **bill or** *(Br)* **note, please?**
¿puede cambiarme un billete de quinientos pesos?
pway-day kam-byar-may oon bee-yay-tay day kee-nyen-tohs pay-sohs

pague en caja
pay at the *(Am)* register(s) or *(Br)* cash desk

¿cómo quiere pagar?
how would you like to pay?

SHOPPING

87

¿tiene algo más chico?
do you have anything smaller?

firme aquí, por favor
could you sign here, please?

¿tiene algún documento de identidad?
do you have any ID?

FOOD

Expressing yourself

where can I buy food around here?
¿dónde puedo comprar comida por aquí?
don-day pway-doh kom-prar kom-ee-da por a-kee

is there a market?
¿hay un mercado?
eye oon mair-kah-doh

is there a bakery around here?
¿hay una panadería por aquí?
eye oo-na pan-a-dair-ee-a por a-kee

I'm looking for the cereals
estoy buscando los cereales
es-toy boos-kan-doh los sair-ray-ah-lays

I'd like five slices of ham
quiero cinco lonchas de jamón
kyair-oh seeng-koh lon-chas day CHa-mohn

I'd like some of that goat's cheese
quiero un poco de ese queso de cabra
kyair-oh oon poh-koh day es-uy kay-soh day kab-ra

it's for four people
es para cuatro personas
es pa-ra kwa-troh pair-soh-nas

about 300 grams
unos trescientos gramos
oo-nos trays-syen-tohs grah-mohs

a kilo of apples, please
un kilo de manzanas
oon kee-loh day man-sah-nas

a bit less/more
un poco menos/más
oon poh-koh may-nohs/mas

can I taste it?
¿puedo probarlo?
pway-doh proh-bar-loh

does it travel well?
¿se conserva bien en el viaje?
say kon-sair-ba byen en el bya-CHay

Understanding

casero	homemade
consumir preferentemente antes de...	best before...
orgánico	organic
productos locales/regionales	local/regional (Am) specialties or (Br) specialities

el café está en el tercer pasillo a la derecha
the coffee's in the third aisle on the right

hay un mercado que abre diariamente hasta la una
there's a market every day until 1 p.m.

hay una tienda de comestibles or (Arg) **un almacén en la esquina que abre hasta tarde**
there's a grocer's or (Am) grocery store on the corner that's open late

CLOTHES

Returning goods is infrequent in Latin America. Always ask for the shop's policy before making a purchase. Exchanges – when allowed – can usually only be made on certain days and times. Always keep the receipt.

Expressing yourself

I'm looking for the menswear section
estoy buscando la sección de caballeros
es-*toy* boos-*kan*-doh la sek-*syohn* day ka-ba-*yair*-ohs

no thanks, I'm just looking
no gracias, sólo estoy mirando
noh *gras*-yas, *soh*-loh es-*toy* mee-*ran*-doh

I take a size 40 *(in shoes)*
calzo 40
kal-soh kwa-ren-tah

I'd like to try the one in the window
me gustaría probarme el de la vitrina *or* vidriera
may goos-ta-ree-a proh-bar-may el day la bee-tree-na/bee-dree-air-a

can I try it on?
¿puedo probármelo?
pway-doh proh-bar-may-loh

where are the fitting rooms?
¿dónde están los probadores?
don-day es-tan los proh-ba-daw-rays

it doesn't fit
no me queda bien
noh may kay-da byen

it's too big/small
me queda grande/chico
may kay-da gran-day/chee-koh

do you have it in another colour?
¿lo tiene en otro color?
loh tyen-ay en oh-troh ko-lor

do you have them in red?
¿los tiene en rojo?
los tyen-ay en ro-CHoh

do you have it in a smaller/bigger size?
¿lo tiene en una talla *or* (Arg) un talle más grande/chico?
loh tyen-ay en oo-na teye-a/oon teye-a mas gran-day/chee-ko

yes, that's fine, I'll take them
sí, me quedan bien, me los llevo
see, may kay-dan byen, may los yay-boh

no, I don't like it
no, no me gusta
noh, noh may goos-ta

I'll think about it
voy a pensarlo
boy a pen-sar-loh

can I return it if it doesn't fit?
¿puedo devolverlo si no me queda bien?
pway-doh day-bol-bair-loh see noh may kay-da byen

this... has a hole in it, can I get a refund?
este… tiene un agujero, ¿puede devolverme el dinero?
es-tay… tyen-eh oon a-goo-CHair-oh, pway-day day-bol-bair-may el dee-nair-oh

Understanding

abierto domingos	open on Sundays
no se aceptan devoluciones	sale items cannot be returned
probadores	fitting rooms
ropa de caballeros	menswear
ropa de damas	ladieswear
ropa infantil	children's clothes
ropa interior	lingerie

hola, ¿puedo ayudarle?	**le queda bien**
hello, can I help you?	it suits you

sólo lo tenemos en azul o en negro
we only have it in blue or black

no nos queda ninguno en esa talla *or (Arg)* **ese talle**
we don't have any left in that size

SOUVENIRS AND GIFTS

Expressing yourself

I'm looking for a present to take home
estoy buscando un regalo para llevar a casa
es-*toy* boos-*kan*-doh oon ray-*gah*-loh *pa*-ra yay-*bar* a ka-sa

I'd like something that's easy to transport
quiero algo que sea fácil de transportar
kyair-oh *al*-goh kay *say*-a *fa*-seel day trans-por-*tar*

it's for a little girl of four
es para una niña de cuatro años
es *pa*-ra *oo*-na *neen*-ya day *kwa*-troh *an*-yohs

could you giftwrap it for me?
¿puede envolvérmelo en papel de regalo?
pway-day em-bol-*bair*-may-loh en pa-*pel* day ray-*gah*-loh

Understanding

fabricado en madera/plata/ oro/lana	made of wood/silver/gold/wool
hecho a mano	handmade
productos artesanales	products made in the traditional way
¿cuánto quiere gastar?	**¿es para regalo?**
how much do you want to spend?	is it for a present?
es típico de la región	
it's typical of the region	

Some informal expressions

¡es un timo/carísimo! that's a rip-off/extortionate!
estoy sin blanca *(or Arg)* **pelado/a** *or (Carib)* **pelao/pelá** I'm broke
cuesta un ojo de la cara it costs a fortune
está tirado de precio it's a real bargain
remate final prices slashed

PHOTOS

The basics

black and white	blanco y negro *blang-koh ee nay-groh*
camera	cámara *kam-a-ra*
colour	color *kol-or*
copy	copia *kop-ya*
digital camera	cámara digital *kam-a-ra dee-CHee-tahl*
disposable camera	cámara desechable *kam-a-ra des-ech-ah-blay*
exposure	exposición *eks-poh-sees-yohn*
film	rollo *ro-yo*
flash	flash *flas*
glossy	con brillo *kon bree-yoh*
matte	mate *mah-tay*
memory card	tarjeta de memoria *tar-CHay-ta day mem-aw-rya*
negative	negativo *nay-ga-tee-boh*
passport photo	foto carné *foh-toh kar-nay*
reprint *(noun)*	copia *kop-ya*
slide	diapositiva *dee-a-pos-ee-tee-ba*
to have photos developed	revelar fotos *re-bel-ar foh-tohs*
to take a photo/photos	sacar *or* tomar una foto/unas fotos *sa-kar/toh-mar oo-na foh-toh/oo-nas foh-tohs*

Expressing yourself

could you take a photo of us, please?
¿nos puede sacar *or* tomar una foto, for favor?
nos pway-day sa-kar/toh-mar oo-na foh-toh, por fa-bor

you just have to press this button
sólo tiene que apretar el botón
soh-loh tyen-ay kay a-pret-ar el bo-tohn

I'd like a 200 ASA colour film
quiero un rollo a color de doscientos ASA
kyair-oh oon ro-yo a ko-lor day dos-syen-tohs a-sa

do you have black and white films?
¿tiene rollos en blanco y negro?
tyen-ay ro-yos en blang-koh ee nay-groh

how much is it to develop a roll/film of 36 photos?
¿cuánto cuesta revelar un rollo de treinta y seis fotos?
kwan-toh kwes-ta re-bel-ar oon ro-yo day trayn-ta ee says foh-tohs

I'd like to have this film developed
¿me puede revelar este rollo?
may pway-day re-bel-ar es-tay ro-yo

I'd like extra copies of some of the photos
quiero hacer copias de algunas fotos
kyair-oh a-sair kop-yas day al-goo-nas foh-tohs

three copies of this one and two of this one
tres copias de ésta y dos de ésta
trays kop-yas day es-ta ee dos day es-ta

can I print my digital photos here?
¿imprimen fotos digitales?
im-pree-men foh-tohs dee-CHee-tah-lays

can you put these photos on a CD for me?
¿me puede grabar estas fotos en un CD?
may pway-day gra-bar es-tas foh-tohs en oon say-day

I've come to pick up my photos
vengo a recoger mis fotos
beng-goh a ray-ko-CHair mees foh-tohs

I have a problem with my camera
mi cámara tiene un problema
mee kam-a-ra tyen-ay oon prob-lay-ma

I don't know what it is
no sé lo que es
noh say loh kay es

the flash doesn't work
el flash no funciona
el flas noh foon-syoh-na

Understanding

formato normal	standard format
fotos en CD	photos on CD
revelado de fotos en una hora	photos developed in one hour
servicio rápido	express service

quizás se le ha acabado la pila
maybe the battery's dead

tenemos una máquina para imprimir fotos digitales
we have a machine for printing digital photos

¿a qué nombre?
what's the name, please?

¿para cuándo las quiere?
when do you want them for?

las podemos revelar en una hora
we can develop them in an hour

las fotos estarán listas el jueves por la tarde
your photos will be ready on Thursday afternoon

PHOTOS

BANKS $

Most banks in Latin America are open weekdays from 9 a.m. to 3 p.m. or 6 p.m., and some are also open on Saturday morning. This varies from one country to another, so check locally. You can withdraw money from the numerous ATMs (**cajeros automáticos**) with an international credit card, which can also be used in most shops, hotels and restaurants (you will probably be asked for ID). Check whether there is an extra charge for paying by credit card. The currency in Argentina, Cuba and Mexico is the **peso**, and in Peru it is the **nuevo sol**.

The basics

ATM	cajero (automático) *ka-CHair-oh (ow-toh-mat-ee-koh)*
bank	banco *bang-koh*
bank account	cuenta bancaria *kwen-ta bang-kah-rya*
banknote *(Br)*, **bill** *(Am)*	billete *bee-yay-tay*
bureau de change	cambio *kam-byoh*
card	tarjeta *tar-CHay-ta*
cashpoint *(Br)*	cajero (automático) *ka-CHair-oh (ow-toh-mat-ee-koh)*
check/cheque	cheque *chek-ay*
coin	moneda *mon-ay-da*
commission	comisión *kom-ee-s-yohn*
counter *(in bank)*	ventanilla *ben-ta-nee-ya*
credit card	tarjeta de crédito *tar-CHay-ta day kred-ee-toh*
exchange *(noun)*	cambio *kam-byoh*
money	dinero *dee-nair-oh*
PIN (number)	número personal *noo-mair-roh pair-soh-nahl*
transfer *(noun)*	transferencia *trans-fair-ens-ya*
traveler's checks/ Travellers Cheques®	cheques de viajero *chek-ays day bya-CHair-oh*
withdrawal	retiro *ray-tee-roh*
to change	cambiar *kam-byar*
to transfer	transferir *trans-fair-eer*

to withdraw money sacar dinero or plata sa-*kar* dee-*nair*-oh/*plah-ta*

Expressing yourself

where I can change some money?
¿dónde puedo cambiar dinero?
don-day pway-doh kam-byar dee-nair-oh

are banks open on Saturdays?
¿los bancos abren los sábados?
los *bang* kohs *ab*-ren los *sab*-a-dohs

I'm looking for an ATM or (Br) **a cashpoint**
estoy buscando un cajero
es *toy booo kan* doh oon ka-*CHair*-oh

I'd like to change $100/£100
quiero cambiar cien dólares/libras
kyair-oh kam-*byar* syen *doh*-la-rays/*lee*-bras

what commission do you charge?
¿qué comisión tienen?
kay kom-ees-*yohn* tyen-en

I'd like to transfer some money
quiero transferir dinero
kyair-oh trans-fair-*eer* dee-*nair*-oh

how long will it take?
¿cuánto tiempo tardará?
kwan-toh *tyem*-poh tar-da-*ra*

I'm waiting for a money order
estoy esperando un giro
es-*toy* es-pair-*an*-doh oon *CHee*-roh

I'd like to report the loss of my credit card
quiero denunciar la pérdida de mi tarjeta de crédito
kyair-oh day-noon-*syar* la *pair*-dee-da day mee tar-*CHay*-ta day *kred*-ee-toh

the ATM or (Br) **cashpoint has swallowed my card**
el cajero se ha tragado mi tarjeta
el ka-*CHair*-oh say a tra-*gah*-doh mee tar-*CHay*-ta

Understanding

idioma
select language required

introduzca su tarjeta
please insert your card

teclee su número personal
please enter your PIN number

retiro con recibo
withdrawal with receipt

retiro sin recibo
withdrawal without receipt

elija importe
please select the amount you require

cajero (temporalmente) fuera de servicio
machine (temporarily) out of service

POST OFFICES

In Latin America you can buy stamps (**sellos** or **estampillas**) at post offices (**Correos**), which are open weekdays from 9 a.m. to 6 p.m. and Saturdays from 9 a.m. to 1 p.m. Supermarkets and souvenir shops sometimes sell stamps too. The price of a stamp depends on the destination, so it's best to ask for a stamp for wherever you are sending your mail. National postal services can be slow and unsafe, so it's best to use them only for postcards – ask about private mail services if you need to send valuables. Always use mailboxes inside post offices rather than those on the street.

The basics

address	dirección *dee-rek-syohn*
airmail	por avión *por ab-yohn*
envelope	sobre *soh-bray*
letter	carta *kar-ta*
mail *(noun)*	correo *ko-RRay-oh*
mailbox *(Am)*	buzón *boo-sohn*
package, parcel	paquete *pa-kay-tay*
post *(Br) (noun)*	correo *ko-RRay-oh*
postbox *(Br)*	buzón *boo-sohn*
postcard	postal *poh-stahl*
postcode *(Br)*	código postal *koh-dee-goh poh-stahl*
post office	(Oficina de) Correos *(of-ee-see-na day) ko-RRay-ohs*
stamp	sello *say-yoh*, estampilla *es-tam-pee-ya*
zip code *(Am)*	código postal *koh-dee-goh poh-stahl*
to mail, *(Br)* **to post**	mandar por correo *man-dar por ko-RRay-oh*
to receive	recibir *re-see-beer*
to send	enviar *en-byar*, mandar *man-dar*

Expressing yourself

is there a post office around here?
¿hay una Oficina de Correos por aquí?
eye oo-na of-ee-see-na day ko-RRay-ohs por a-kee

is there *(Am)* **a mailbox** *or (Br)* **a postbox near here?**
¿hay un buzón por aquí cerca?
*eye oon boo-**sohn** por a-**kee** sair-ka*

is the post office open on Saturdays?
¿el Correo abre los sábados?
*el ko-**RRay**-oh ab-ray los sab-a-dohs*

what time does the post office close?
¿a qué hora cierra el Correo?
*a kay **aw**-ra syaiRR-a el ko-**RRay**-o*

how much is a stamp for the USA/the UK ?
¿cuánto cuesta un sello *or* una estampilla para los Estados Unidos/el Reino Unido?
*kwan-toh **kwes**-ta oon **say**-yoh/**oo**-na es-tam-**pee**-ya **pa**-ra los es-**tah**-dohs oo-nee-dohs/el **ray**-noh oo-**nee**-doh*

I'd like… stamps for the USA/the UK, please
por favor, quiero… sellos *or* estampillas para los Estados Unidos/el Reino Unido
*por fa-**bor**, **kyair**-oh… **say**-yohs/es-tam-**pee**-yas **pa**-ra los es-**tah**-dohs oo-nee-dohs/el **ray**-noh oo-**nee**-doh*

where can I buy envelopes?
¿dónde venden sobres?
*don-day **ben**-den **soh**-brays*

I'd like to send this package/parcel to Boston/London
quiero enviar este paquete a Boston/Londres
*kyair-oh en-byur es-tay pa-**kay**-tay a **bos**-ton/**lon**-drays*

how long will it take to arrive?
¿cuánto tiempo tardará en llegar?
*kwan-toh **tyem**-poh tar-da-**ra** en yay-**gar***

is there any mail for me?
¿tengo correo?
*teng-goh ko-**RRay**-oh*

my address is …
mi dirección es…
*mee dee-rek-**syohn** es …*

In Latin America, the house number is given after the street name. So, for example, "23 Simón Bolívar Street" would be written as "calle Simón Bolívar 23", or abbreviated to "c/ Simón Bolívar 23". For apartments, the floor and door numbers are often given in the address. So **4o** refers to the floor (**cuarto piso**, *(Am)* fifth floor, *(Br)* fourth floor), and **A** to the door (**puerta A**), or **4°1** refers to the floor and apartment number (**cuarto piso, departamento uno**). But be aware that floor numbering can be misleading as many buildings have a **planta baja** ((Am) first floor, *(Br)* ground floor) and a mezzanine, abbreviated to **MZ**. This means that the **primer piso** may actually be what Americans consider the third floor and the British call the second floor! A full address might read as follows: **c/ Simón Bolívar 23, 4o A, 22000 Lima** or **c/ Simón Bolívar 23, 4°1, 22000 Lima**.

Understanding

destinatario	recipient
frágil	fragile
recolección mañanas	first collection
recolección tardes	afternoon collection
remitente	sender
última recolección	last collection

¿cuál es su dirección?	**tardará entre tres y cinco días**
what's your address?	it'll take between three and five days

Understanding Latin American addresses

Some common abbreviations are **c/** for calle (street), **Pza.** for plaza (square), **Av.** for avenida (avenue), **Po** for paseo (avenue), **Ctra** for carretera (road) and **s/n** for sin número (when the address doesn't have a house number). Peru uses **Ov.** for óvalo ((Am) traffic circle, *(Br)* roundabout) and **Jr**. for jirón (street). Mexico and Peru have **urbanizaciones** (urban areas) abbreviated to **Urb**. **Avenidas** are generally two-way roads; Mexico City has seven-lane avenues called **ejes**.

INTERNET CAFÉS AND E-MAIL

www

There are more and more Internet cafés in Latin America, and it is becoming increasingly common to exchange e-mail addresses with people. Spanish speakers use the international (QWERTY) keyboard.

The *at* sign is called an **arroba** (*a-RRoh-ba*), a *dot* is a **punto** (*poon-toh*) and a *dash* is a **guión** (*gee-yohn*). **Todo junto** (*toh-doh CHoon-toh*) means that a part of the address is all one word. So, for example, the address **mariajimenez@wanadoo.pe** would be given as "**maria jimenez (todo junto) arroba wanadoo punto pe**" (*ma-ree-a CHee-may-nes toh-doh CHoon-toh a-RRoh-ba wa-na-doo poon-toh pay*).

The basics

computer	computadora *kom-poo-ta-daw-ra*
e-mail	email *ee-mayl*
e-mail address	(dirección de) email *(dee-rek-syohn day) ee-mayl*
Internet café	cibercafé *see-bair-ka-fay*
key	tecla *tek-la*
keyboard	teclado *tek-lah-doh*
to copy	copiar *cop-yar*
to cut	cortar *kor-tar*
to delete	eliminar *ay-lee-mee-nar*
to download	bajar *ba-CHar*, descargar *des-kar-gar*
to e-mail somebody	mandar un email a alguien *man-dar oon ee-mayl a al-gyen*
to paste	pegar *peg-ar*
to receive	recibir *res-ee-beer*
to save	guardar *gwar-dar*
to send an e-mail	enviar un email *en-byar*

Expressing yourself

is there an Internet café near here?
¿hay un cibercafé por aquí?
eye oon see-bair-ka-fay por a-kee

do you have an e-mail address?
¿tienes correo electrónico?
tyen-es ko-RRay-oh ay-lek-tron-ee-koh

how do I get online?
¿cómo entro en Internet?
koh-moh en-troh en een-tair-net

I'd just like to check my e-mails
sólo quiero mirar or (Chil, Peru) chequear or (Mex) checar mi correo
soh-loh kyair-oh mee-rar/chek-ay-ar/chek-ar mee ko-RRay-oh

can you help me? I'm not sure what to do
¿puede ayudarme? no sé bien lo que hay que hacer
pway-day eye-oo-dar-may. noh say byen loh kay eye kay a-sair

there's something wrong with the computer, it's frozen
algo le pasa a la computadora, se ha bloqueado
al-goh lay pah-sa a la kom-poo-ta-daw-ra, say a blok-ay-ah-do

how much will it be for half an hour?
¿cuánto cuesta la media hora?
kwan-toh kwes-ta la med-ya aw-ra

it's not working
no funciona
noh foon-syoh-na

when do I pay?
¿cuándo se paga?
kwan-doh say pa-ga

can I make a phone call via the Internet?
¿se puede llamar por teléfono a través de Internet?
say pway-day yam-ar a tra-bes day een-tair-net

Understanding

bandeja de entrada	inbox
bandeja de salida	outbox

WWW

escriba su palabra clave para conectarse
enter your password to log on

pregunte si no sabe lo que hay que hacer
just ask if you're not sure what to do

tiene que esperar unos veinte minutos
you'll have to wait for 20 minutes or so

Public telephones are often open, which can make things difficult if you have to contend with street noise etc. Note that you cannot be called back as payphones do not have their own numbers. Many phones now take phonecards (**tarjetas telefónicas**), although most still accept coins (**monedas**).

Phonecards are sold in newspaper kiosks (**quioscos**). Prepaid cards (**tarjetas prepago**) are becoming increasingly common, and can be used from private phones as well as phonebooths. They also tend to offer better value on international calls. In Argentina and Peru you'll find **locutorios** (communication centres with phones, Internet access etc), which offer good value for international calls.

To call the USA from Latin America, you need to dial 00 1 followed by the area code and phone number. To call the UK, dial 00 44 followed by the area code (minus the first zero) and phone number.

The basics

answering machine	contestador (automático) kon-tes-ta-**dor** ow-toh-**ma**-tee-koh
call (noun)	llamada yam-**ah**-da
cellphone (Am)	celular sel-oo-**lar**
directory assistance (Am), **directory enquiries** (Br)	información telefónica ecn for-mas-**yohn** te-lay-**fon**-ee-ka
directory enquiries (Br)	información telefónica een-for-mas-**yohn** te-lay-**fon**-ee-ka
hello	(when answering) aló a-**loh**, (Arg) hola oh-la, (Mex) bueno bway-noh; (when calling) aló a-**lo**, (Arg) hola oh-la
international call	llamada internacional yam-**ah**-da een-tair-nas-yoh-**nahl**
local call	llamada local yam-**ah**-da loh-**kahl**

message	mensaje *men*-sa-*CHay*, (*Peru*) recado *ray*-ka-do
mobile (phone) (*Br*)	celular sel-oo-*lar*
national call (*Br*)	llamada nacional yam-*ah*-da nas-yoh-*nal*
phone (*noun*)	teléfono te-*lay*-fon-oh
phone book	guía telefónica *gee*-a te-lay-*fon*-ee-ka
phone booth	cabina telefónica ka-*bee*-na te-lay-*fon*-ee-ka, (*Arg*) locutorio lok-oo-*taw*-ryo
phone call	llamada telefónica yam-*ah*-da
phone number	número de teléfono *noo*-mair-oh day te-*lay*-fon-oh
phonecard	tarjeta telefónica tar-*CHay*-ta te-lay-*fon*-ee-ka
prepaid card	(*for payphone*) tarjeta telefónica tar-*CHay*-ta te-lay-*fon*-ee-ka; (*Am*) (*for cellphone*) tarjeta prepago tar-*CHay*-ta pray-*pah*-goh
ringtone	señal de llamada sen-*yahl* day yam-*ah*-da
telephone	teléfono te-*lay*-fon-oh
top-up card (*Br*)	tarjeta prepago tar-*CHay*-ta pray-*pah*-goh
Yellow Pages®	Páginas Amarillas® pa-*CHee*-nas a-ma-*ree*-yas
to call	llamar yam-*ar*
to call somebody	llamar a alguien yam-*ar* a al-gyen
to phone	telefonear te-lay-fon-ay-*ar*

Expressing yourself

where can I buy a phonecard?
¿dónde puedo comprar una tarjeta telefónica?
don-day *pway*-doh kom-*prar* oo-na tar-*CHay*-ta te-lay-*fon*-ee-ka

a ...-peso (*Am*) **prepaid card** or (*Br*) **top-up card, please**
una tarjeta prepago de... pesos
oo-na tar-*CHay*-ta pray-*pah*-goh day... *pay*-sohs, por fa-*bor*

I'd like to make (*Am*) **a collect call** or (*Br*) **a reverse-charge call**
quisiera hacer una llamada a cobro or cargo revertido or (*Mex*) por cobrar
kees-*yair*-a a-*sair* oo-na yam-*ah*-da a *kob*-roh/*kar*-go ray-bair-*tee*-doh/por kob-*rar*

is there a phone booth near here, please?
perdone ¿hay una cabina or (Arg) un locutorio por aquí cerca?
pair-doh-nay, eye oo-na ka-bee-na/oon lok-oo-taw-ryo por a-kee sair-ka

can I plug my phone in here to recharge it?
¿puedo recargar mi teléfono en este enchufe?
pway-doh ray-kar-gar mee te-lay-fon-oh en es-tay en-choo-fay

do you have (Am) **a cellphone number** or (Br) **a mobile number?**
¿tienes número de celular?
tyen-es noo-mair-oh day sel-oo-lar

where can I contact you?
¿dónde puedo contactarte?
don-day pway-doh kon-tak-tar-tay

did you get my message?
¿recibiste mi mensaje or (Peru) recado?
res-ee-bees-tay mee men-sa-CHay/ray-ka-do

Understanding

acepta monedas de...   takes... coins

el número marcado no existe
the number you have dialled has not been recognized

pulse (la tecla) asterisco/numeral
please press the star/hash key

MAKING A CALL

Expressing yourself

hello, this is David Brown (speaking)
aló or (Arg) hola, soy David Brown
a-loh/oh-la, soy david brown

hello, could I speak to ..., please?
aló or (Arg) hola, ¿puedo hablar con... por favor?
a-loh/oh-la, pway-do ab-lar kon... por fa-bor

hello, is that María?
aló or (Arg) hola, ¿hablo con María?
a-loh/oh-la, ab-lo kon ma-ree-a

do you speak English?
¿hablas inglés?
ab-las eeng-glays

could you speak more slowly, please?
¿puede hablar más despacio, por favor?
pway-day ab-lar mas des-pas-yo, por fa-bor

I can't hear you, could you speak up, please?
no le oigo, ¿puede hablar más alto, por favor?
noh lay oy-goh, pway-day ab-lar mas al-toh, por fa-bor

could you tell him/her I called?
¿puede decirle que lo/la he llamado?
pway-day des-eer-lay kay loh/la ay yam-ah-doh

could you ask him/her to call me back?
¿puede decirle que me llame?
pway-day des-eer-lay kay may yah-may

my name is… and my number is…
soy… y mi número es el…
soy… ee mee noo-mair-oh es el…

do you know when he/she might be available?
¿sabe cuándo podré hablar con él/ella?
sab-ay kwan-doh pod-ray ab-lar kon el/ay-yu

thank you, goodbye	**I'll call back later**
gracias, adiós	llamaré más tarde
gras-yas, ad-yohs	*yam-a-ray mas tar-day*

Understanding

¿de parte de quién?
who's calling?

no está en este momento
he's/she's not here at the moment

¿quiere dejar algún mensaje or (Peru) **recado?**
do you want to leave a message?

le diré que ha llamado
I'll tell him/her you called

espere
hold on

le diré que lo/a llame
I'll ask him/her to call you back

ya se lo/la paso
I'll just hand you over to him/her

PROBLEMS

Expressing yourself

I don't know the area code
no sé el código de área or (Mex) la clave LADA
noh say el **koh**-dee-goh day **a**-ray-a/la **kla**-bay **lah**-da

it's (Am) **busy** or (Br) **engaged**
está ocupado
es-**ta** o-koo-**pah**-doh

there's no reply
no contesta
noh kon-**tes**-ta

I couldn't get through to him
no pude hablar con él
noh **poo**-day ab-**lar** kon el

I can't get a signal
no tengo señal
noh **teng**-goh sen-**yahl**

I don't have (Am) **many minutes** or (Br) **much credit left on my phone**
se me está terminando el crédito or no tengo saldo en el teléfono
say may es-**ta** tair-mee-**nan**-do el **cred**-ee-toh/no **teng**-goh **sal**-doh en el tel-**ay**-fon-oh

the reception's really bad
se oye muy mal
say **oy**-ay mwee mal

we're about to get cut off
se va a cortar
say ba a kor-**tar**

Understanding

te oigo muy mal
I can hardly hear you

se me ha cortado
I got cut off

se ha equivocado de número
you've got the wrong number

Common abbreviations

Tel. (trabajo) work (number)
Tel. (casa) home (number)
Tel. Cel. *(Am)* cellphone *or (Br)* mobile (number)

Some informal expressions

dar un telefonazo to make a call
colgarle el teléfono a alguien to hang up on somebody

TELEPHONE

HEALTH

The basics

allergy	alergia *al-air-CHee-ya*
ambulance	ambulancia *am-boo-lans-ya*
aspirin	aspirina *as-pee-ree-na*
Band-Aid® *(Am)*	curita *koo-ree-ta*
blood	sangre *sang-gray*
broken	roto *roh-toh*
casualty (department) *(Br)*	urgencias *oor-CHens-yas*
chemist's *(Br)*	farmacia *far-mas-ya*
condom	condón *kon-dohn*
dentist	dentista *den-tees-ta*
diarrhoea	diarrea *dee-a-RRay-a*
doctor	médico *med-ee-koh*
emergency room *(Am)*	urgencias *oor-CHens-yas*
food poisoning	intoxicación alimentaria *een-tok-see-kas-yohn a-lee-men-tah-rya*
GP	médico general *or* de cabecera *med-ee-koh CHen-ay-rahl/day ka-bay-sair-a*
gynaecologist	ginecólogo *CHee-nay-kol-oh-goh*
hospital	hospital *os-pee-tal*
infection	infección *een-fek-syohn*
medicine	medicina *med-ee-see-na*, *(Arg)* remedio *ray-may-dee-oh*
migraine	migraña *mee-gran-ya*

HEALTH

painkiller	analgésico an-al-**CHes**-ee-koh
period	periodo pair-ee-**oh**-doh, (Carib, Peru) regla **ray**-gla
pharmacy	farmacia far-**mas**-ya
pimple (Am)	grano **grah**-noh
plaster (Br)	curita koo-**ree**-ta
primary care physician (Am)	médico general or de cabecera **med**-ee-koh CHen-ay-**rahl**/day ka-bay-**sair**-a
rash	erupción ay-roop-**syohn**
rubbing alcohol (Am)	alcohol al-koh-**ol**
spot (Br)	grano **grah**-noh
sunburn	quemadura de sol kay-ma-**doo**-ra day sol
surgical spirit (Br)	alcohol al-koh-**ol**
tablet	pastilla pas-**tee**-ya
temperature	fiebre **fyeb**-ray
vaccination	vacuna ba-**koo**-na
x-ray	rayos-X **reye**-ohs **ek**-ees
to disinfect	desinfectar des-een-fek-**tar**
to faint	desmayarse des-meye-**ar**-say
to vomit (verb)	vomitar bom-ee-**tar**

Expressing yourself

does anyone have an aspirin/a tampon/(Am) a BandAid® or (Br) a plaster?
¿tiene alguien una aspirina/un tampon/una curita?
tyen-ay **al**-gyen oo-na as-pee-**ree**-na/oon tam-**pohn**/oo-na koo-**ree**-ta

I need to see a doctor
necesito ver a un médico
nes-ay-**see**-toh bair a oon **med**-ee-koh

where can I find a doctor?
¿dónde hay un médico?
don-day eye oon **med**-ee-koh

I'd like to make an appointment for today
quisiera pedir or (Carib) hacer or (Peru) sacar una cita para hoy
kees-**yair**-a pe-**deer**/a-**sair**/sa-**kar** oo-na **see**-ta **pa**-ra oy

as soon as possible
lo antes posible
loh an-tes po-see-blay

no, it doesn't matter
no, no importa
noh, noh eem-por-ta

can you send an ambulance to...
¿puede mandar una ambulancia a...?
pway-day man-dar oo-na am-boo-lan-sya a...

I've broken my glasses
se me han roto los lentes *or (Carib)* espejuelos
say may an roh-toh los len-tays/es-pay-CHoo-ay-lohs

I've lost a contact lens
he perdido un lente de contacto
ay pair-dee-doh oon len-tay day kon-tak-toh

Understanding

consulta médica, *(Arg, Peru)* **consultorio médico**	doctor's *(Am)* office *or (Br)* surgery
oficina del médico	doctor's *(Am)* office *or (Br)* surgery
receta	prescription
remedio *(Arg)*	medicine
urgencias	*(Am)* emergency room, *(Br)* casualty (department)

no hay más citas hasta el jueves
there are no available appointments until Thursday

¿le viene bien el viernes a las dos?
is Friday at 2 p.m. ok?

AT THE DOCTOR'S OR THE HOSPITAL

Expressing yourself

I have an appointment with Dr...
tengo una cita con el doctor...
teng-goh oo-na see-ta kon el dok-tor...

HEALTH

I don't feel very well
no me siento muy bien
*noh may **syen**-toh mwee byen*

I feel very weak
me siento muy débil
*may **syen**-toh mwee **day**-beel*

I have a headache
me duele la cabeza
*may **dway**-lay la ka-**bay**-sa*

I have a sore throat
me duele la garganta
*may **dway**-lay la gar-**gan**-ta*

I have (a) toothache
tengo dolor de muelas
*teng-goh dol-**or** day **mway**-las/*

I have a temperature
tengo fiebre
*teng-goh **fyeb**-ray*

it hurts
duele
dway-lay

it hurts here
me duele aquí
*may **dway**-lay a-**kee***

I feel sick or (Am) **nauseous**
tengo ganas de vomitar
*teng-goh **gan**-as day bom-ee-**tar***

it itches
me pica
*may **pee**-ka*

I've been bitten/stung by…
me ha mordido/picado un…
*may a mor-**dee**-doh/pee-**kah**-doh oon…*

I blacked out
he tenido un desmayo
*ay te-**nee**-doh oon des-**meye**-oh*

I've lost a filling
se me ha caído un empaste
*say may a ka-**ee**-doh oon em-**pas**-tay*

my back hurts
me duele la espalda
*may **dway**-lay la es-**pal**-da*

I've twisted my ankle
me he torcido el tobillo
*may hay tor-**ree** doh ul tob ee yoh*

I fell and hurt my back
me he caído y me he hecho daño en la espalda
*may ay keye-**ee**-doh ee may ay **ech**-oh **dan**-yoh en la es-**pal**-da*

I don't know what it is
no sé lo que es
noh say loh kay es

it's never happened to me before
nunca me ha pasado antes
***noong**-ka may a pas-**ah**-doh **an**-tes*

it started last night
empezó anoche
*em-pes-**oh** a-**noch**-ay*

it's got worse
ha empeorado
*a em-pay-oh-**rah**-doh*

I've felt like this for three days
me siento así desde hace tres días
may syen-toh a-see dez-day a-say trays dee-as

I've been on antibiotics for a week and I'm not getting any better
llevo dos semanas con antibióticos y no mejoro
yay-boh dos say-mah-nas kon an-tee-byot-ee-kohs ee noh may-CHor-oh

I have asthma
tengo asma
teng-goh as-ma

I have a heart condition
sufro *or* padezco del corazón
soo-froh/pa-des-koh del ko-ra-sohn

I'm on the pill
estoy tomando la píldora
es-toy to-man-doh la peel-daw-ra

I'm... months pregnant
estoy embarazada de... meses
es-toy em-ba-ra-sah-da day... may-says

I'm allergic to penicillin
soy alérgico a la penicilina
soy a-lair-CHee-koh a la pen-ee-see-lee-na

is it serious?
¿es grave?
es grah-bay

is it contagious?
¿es contagioso?
es kon-taCH-yoh-soh

how is he/she?
¿cómo está?
koh-moh es-ta

how much do I owe you?
¿cuánto le debo?
kwan-toh lay day-boh

can I have a receipt so I can get the money refunded?
¿me da un recibo para que me devuelvan el dinero?
may da oon ray-see-boh pa-ra kay may day-bwel-ban el dee-nair-oh

Understanding

por favor, pase a la sala de espera
take a seat in the waiting room, please

acuéstese *or* recuéstese, por favor
lie down, please

HEALTH

115

respire hondo
take a deep breath

¿dónde le duele?
where does it hurt?

¿es usted alérgico a…?
are you allergic to…?

¿se ha vacunado contra…
have you been vaccinated against…?

¿está tomando otra medicación?
are you taking any other medication?

le voy a hacer una receta
I'm going to write you a prescription

se le pasará en unos días
it should clear up in a few days

se le sanará pronto
it should heal quickly

habrá que operarle
you're going to need an operation

vuelva a verme dentro de una semana
come back and see me in a week

AT THE PHARMACY

Expressing yourself

I'd like a box of (Am) **Band-Aids®** or (Br) **plasters, please**
quisiera una caja de curitas, por favor
kees-yair-a oo-na ka-CHa day koo-ree-tas, por fa-bor

could I have something for a bad cold?
¿me da algo para un resfriado or (Arg) resfrío fuerte?
may dah al-goh pa-ra oon res-free-ah-doh/res-free-oh fwair-tay

I need something for a cough
necesito algo para la tos
nes-ay-see-toh al-goh pa-ra la tos

I'm allergic to aspirin
soy alérgico a la aspirina
soy a-lair-CHee-koh a la as-pee-ree-na

I need the morning-after pill
necesito la píldora del día después
nes-ay-see-toh la peel-daw-ra del dee-a des-pways

I'd like to try a homeopathic remedy
quisiera probar un remedio homeopático
kees-yair-a proh-bar oon ray-med-yoh oh-may-oh-pat-ee-koh

I'd like a bottle of solution for soft contact lenses
quisiera un frasco de líquido para lentes de contacto blandos
kees-yair-a oon fras-koh day lee-kee-doh pa-ra len-tays day kon-tak-toh blan-dohs

---

Understanding

aplicar	apply
cápsula	capsule
contraindicaciones	contra-indications
crema	cream
en ayunas	on an empty stomach
en polvo	powdered
jarabe	syrup
pastilla	tablet
polvo	powder
pomada	ointment
posibles efectos secundarios	possible side effects
sólo con receta médica	available on prescription only
supositorios	suppositories
tableta	tablet
tres veces al día antes de las comidas	three times a day before meals

---

Some informal expressions
tener una tos de perro to have a hacking cough
estar súper resfriado or *(Carib)* **tener una monga terrible** to have a terrible cold
no estoy muy católico I don't feel too good

PROBLEMS AND EMERGENCIES

Be wary of pickpockets and bag snatchers, especially in cities and at popular tourist sites. In an emergency of any kind in Peru, dial 116 (**bomberos**). If it is specifically a police matter, for example if you lose something or have something stolen, go to the nearest police station (**comisaría**) or dial 105. Police officers in Peru are recognizable by their dark green uniforms, though in many areas security is handled by **serenos** in blue uniforms. In any emergency in Mexico call 5250-0123, a 24-hour hotline for tourists providing immediate assistance and general information. For emergencies in Mexico City you can also dial 060, or 066 in other parts of the country. In Mexico City dial 5346-8733, -8730, -8154 or -8734 for police with English translation. In Cuba you will find tourist police in the streets. In Argentina, dial 911 in any emergency.

The basics

accident	accidente *ak-see-den-tay*
ambulance	ambulancia *am-boo-lan-sya*
broken	roto *roh toh*
coastguard	guardacostas *gwar-da-kos-tas*
disabled	minusválido *mee noos bal-ee-doh*
doctor	médico *med-ee-koh*
emergency	urgencia *oor-CHen-sya*
fire	fuego *fway-goh*
fire brigade (*Br*), fire department (*Am*)	bomberos *bom-bair-ohs*
hospital	hospital *os-pee-tahl*
ill	enfermo *en-fair-moh*
injured	herido *e-ree-doh*
police	policía *pol-ee-see-a*
sick (*Am*)	enfermo *en-fair-moh*

!

help!
¡socorro!
so-**koRR**-oh

fire!
¡fuego!
fway-goh

be careful!
¡cuidado!
kwee-**dah**-doh

can you help me?
¿puede ayudarme?
pway-day eye oo-**dar**-may

it's an emergency!
¡es una urgencia!
es **oo**-na oor-**CHen**-sya

there's been an accident
ha habido un accidente
a a-**bee**-doh oon ak-see-**den**-tay

he's drowning, get help!
se está ahogando, ¡ayuda!
say es-**ta** a-oh-**gan**-doh, eye **oo**-da

could I borrow your phone, please?
¿puedo usar su teléfono?
pway-doh oo-**sar** soo tel-**ay**-foh-noh

does anyone here speak English?
¿alguien habla inglés?
al-gyen **ab**-la eeng-**glays**

I need to contact the American/British consulate
tengo que ponerme en contacto con el consulado americano/británico
teng-go kay pon-**air**-may en kon-**tak**-toh kon el kon-soo-**lah**-doh a-mair-ee-kah-noh/bree-**tan**-ee-koh

where's the nearest police station?
¿dónde está la comisaría más cercana?
don-day es-**ta** la kom-ee-sa-**ree**-a mas sair-**kah**-na

what do I have to do?
¿qué tengo que hacer?
kay **teng**-goh kay a-**sair**

my bag's been snatched
me han robado la cartera or (Mex) bolsa
may han roh-**bah**-doh la kar-**tair**-a/**bol**-sa

my passport/credit card has been stolen
me han robado el pasaporte/ la tarjeta de crédito
may an roh-**bah**-doh el pa-sa-**por**-tay/la tar-**CHay**-ta day **kred**-ee-toh

I've lost…
he perdido…
ay pair-dee-doh…

I've been attacked
he sufrido una agresión
ay soo-free-doh oona ag-res-yohn

my son/daughter is missing
mi hijo/hija se ha perdido
mee ee-CHoh/ee-CHa say a pair-dee-doh

there's a man following me
un hombre me está siguiendo
oon om-bray may es-ta see-gyen-doh

my car's been towed away
la grúa se ha llevado mi coche *or (Arg)* auto *or (Carib, Mex, Peru)* carro
la groo-a say a yay-bah-doh mee ko-chay/ow-to/ka-RRo

my car's broken down
he tenido un problema con el coche *or (Arg)* auto *or (Carib, Mex, Peru)* carro
ay ten-ee-doh oon prob-lay-ma kon el ko-chay/ow-to/ka-RRo

my car's been broken into
me han entrado en el coche *or (Arg)* auto *or (Carib, Mex, Peru)* carro
may an en-trah-doh en el ko-chay/ow-to/ka-RRo

can you keep an eye on my things for a minute?
¿podría cuidarme las cosas un momentito?
pod-ree-a kwee-dar-may las koh-sas oon moh-men tee-toh

Understanding

cuidado con el perro	beware of the dog
dañado *(Carib)*	out of order
descompuesto	out of order
malogrado *(Peru)*	out of order
objetos perdidos	*(Am)* lost-and-found, *(Br)* lost property
salida de emergencia	emergency exit
salvamento de montaña	mountain rescue
servicio de averías *or* **reparaciones**	*(Am)* emergency road service, *(Br)* breakdown service

POLICE

Expressing yourself

I want to report something stolen
quiero denunciar un robo
kyair-oh day-noon-syar oon roh-boh

I need a document from the police for my insurance company
necesito una copia de la denuncia para mi compañía de seguros
ne-say-see-toh oo-na kop-ya day la day-noon-sya pa-ra mee kom-pan-yee-a day say-goo-rohs

Understanding

Filling out forms

apellido surname
nombre first name
dirección address
código postal *(Am)* zip code, *(Br)* postcode
país country
nacionalidad nationality
fecha de nacimiento date of birth
lugar de nacimiento place of birth
edad age
sexo sex
duración de la estancia *or* **estadía** duration of stay
fecha de llegada/salida arrival/departure date
profesión occupation
número de pasaporte passport number

¿qué falta?
what's missing?

¿dónde se aloja?
where are you staying?

¿cuándo ocurrió?
when did this happen?

¿puede describirlo/la?
can you describe him *or* her *or* it?

PROBLEMS, EMERGENCIES

121

¿puede rellenar *(Arg, Peru)* **este formulario** or *(Carib, Mex)* **forma, por favor?**
would you fill out this form, please?

¿puede firmar aquí, por favor?
would you sign here, please?

este producto tiene que pagar impuestos
there's customs duty to pay on this item

¿puede abrir esta maleta or *(Arg)* **valija, por favor?**
would you open this bag, please?

Some informal expressions

(Arg, Peru) **cana,** *(Mex)* **bote** slammer, clink
(Arg) **chorro,** *(Carib)* **pillo,** *(Mex)* **ratero,** *(Peru)* **choro** thief, crook
me han mangado la cartera, *(Arg)* **me afanaron la billetera** my wallet's been pinched!
(Arg) **cana,** *(Mex)* **poli,** *(Peru)* **tombo** cop

TIME AND DATE

The basics

after	después *des-***pways**
already	ya *yah*
always	siempre *syem-pray*
at lunchtime	a mediodía *a med-yoh-***dee**-*a*
at the beginning/end of	al principio/final de *al preen-***seep**-*yoh/fee-***nahl** *day*
at the moment	en este momento *en es-tay moh-men toh*
before	antes *an-tays*
between... and...	entre... y... *en tray,,, ee...*
day	día *dee-a*
during	durante *doo-ran-tay*
early	temprano *tem-prah-noh*
evening	noche *no-chay*; (before dark) tarde *tar-day*
for a long time	durante mucho tiempo *doo-ran-tay moo-choh tyem-poh*
from... to	desde... hasta... *dez-day... as-ta...*
from time to time	de vez en cuando *day bes en ***kwan**-*doh*
immediately	enseguida *en-say-***gee**-*da*
in a little while	dentro de poco *den-troh day poh-koh*
in the middle of	en mitad de *en mee-***tad** *day*
last	último *ool-tee-moh*
late	tarde *tar-day*
morning	mañana *man-***yah**-*na*
month	mes *mes*
never	nunca *noong-ka*
next	próximo *prok-see-moh*
night	noche *no-chay*
not yet	todavía no *toh-da-***bee**-*a noh*
now	ahora *a-***aw**-*ra*
occasionally	de vez en cuando *day bes en ***kwan**-*doh*
often	a menudo *a may-***noo**-*doh*
rarely	raramente *rah-ra-***men**-*tay*
recently	recientemente *rays-yen-tay-***men**-*tay*

right away	enseguida en-say-**gee**-da
since	desde **dez**-day
sometimes	a veces a **bes**-ays
soon	pronto **pron**-toh
still	todavía toh-da-**bee**-a
until	hasta **as**-ta
week	semana say-**mah**-na
weekend	fin de semana feen day say-**mah**-na
year	año **an**-yoh

Expressing yourself

see you soon!
¡hasta pronto!
as-ta **pron**-*toh*

see you later!
¡hasta luego!
as-ta **lway**-*goh*

see you on Monday!
¡hasta el lunes!
as-ta el **loo**-*nes*

have a good weekend!
¡buen fin de semana!
*bwen feen day say-**mah**-na*

I haven't been there yet
no he estado allí todavía
*noh ay es-**tah**-doh a-yee toh-da-**bee**-a*

I have plenty of time
tengo tiempo de sobra or todo el tiempo del mundo
*teng-goh tyem-poh day **soh**-bra/toh-doh el tyem-poh del moon-doh*

I haven't had time to ...
no he tenido tiempo de...
noh ay ten-ee-doh tyem-poh day...

just a minute, please
un minuto, por favor
*oon mee-**noo**-toh, por fa-**bor***

I'm in a rush
estoy apurado/a, *(Peru)* tengo prisa
*es-**toy** a-poo-**ra**-doh/a-poo-**rah**-da/**teng**-goh **pree**-sa*

hurry up!
(Arg, Peru) ¡apura!, *(Carib)* ¡avanza!, *(Mex)* ¡ándale!
*a-**poo**-ra/a-**ban**-sa/an-da-lay*

I waited ages
esperé horas
*es-pair-**ay** aw-ras*

I had a late night
me acosté tarde
*may a-kos-**tay** tar-day*

I got up very early
me he levantado temprano
may ay leb-an-tah-doh tem-prah-noh

I have to get up early tomorrow to catch my plane
mañana tengo que levantarme temprano para tomar *or (Carib)* coger
el avión
man-yah-na teng-goh kay leb-an-tar-may tem-prah-noh pa-ra toh-mar/ko-CHair el ab-yohn

THE DATE

How to write dates

The following examples show how dates are written in Spanish:

Tuesday, 5 August 2005	**martes 5 de agosto de 2007**, often shortened to **martes 5/8/2007** ("martes cinco de agosto de dos mil siete") -- the order is "day/month/year" as in Britain, rather than the American style of "month/day/year"
2 January 2007	**el dos de enero de dos mil siete**
in June 2007	**en junio de dos mil siete**
from 1999 to 2003	**de mil novecientos noventa y nueve a dos mil tres**
in the 21st century	**en el siglo veintiuno**
200 BC	**200 aC** *or* **200 a. de C.** ("...antes de Cristo)
200 AD	**200 dC** *or* **200 d. de C.** ("...después de Cristo")

The basics

...ago	hace... *a-say*...
in two days' time	dentro de dos días *den-troh day dos dee-as*
last night	anoche *a-no-chay*
the day after tomorrow	pasado mañana *pa-sah-doh man-yah-na*

the day before yesterday	anteayer *an-tay eye-air*
today	hoy *oy*
tomorrow	mañana *man-yah-na*
tomorrow morning/ afternoon/evening	mañana por or en or (Arg) a la mañana/tarde/ noche *man-yah-na por/en/a la man-yah-na/ tar-day/no-chay*
yesterday	ayer *eye-air*
yesterday morning/ afternoon/evening	ayer por or en or (Arg) a la mañana/tarde/ noche *eye-air por/en/a la man-yah-na/tar-day/ no-chay*

Expressing yourself

I was born in 1975
nací en 1975
na-see en meel no-bay-syen-tohs set-en-ta ee seeng-koh

I came here a few years ago
vine aquí hace unos años
bee-nay a-kee a-say oo-nos an-yohs

I spent a month in Mexcio last summer
pasé un mes en México el verano pasado
pa-say oon mes en meCH-ee-koh el bair-ah-noh pas-ah-doh

I was here last year at the same time
el año pasado estuve aquí en la misma epoca
el an-yoh pas-ah-doh es-too-bay a-kee en la meez-ma ay-poh-ka

what's today's date?
¿qué fecha es hoy?
kay fe-cha es oy

what day is it today?
¿qué día es hoy?
kay dee-a es oy

it's (Am) **May 1st** or (Br) **the 1st of May**
es primero de mayo
es pree-mair-oh day meye-oh

I'm staying until Sunday
me quedo hasta el domingo
may kay-doh as-ta el do-meeng-goh

we're leaving tomorrow
nos vamos mañana
nos bah-mos man-yah-na

we only have 4 days left
sólo nos quedan cuatro días
*soh-*loh nos *kay-*dan *kwat-*roh *dee-*as

una vez/dos veces	once/twice
tres veces a la hora/al día	three times an hour/a day
todos los días	every day
todos los lunes	every Monday

sale cada dos semanas
comes out every two weeks

fue construido a mediados del siglo diecinueve
it was built in the mid-nineteenth century

aquí viene mucha gente en verano
it gets very busy here in the summer

¿cuándo se va?
when are you leaving?

¿cuánto tiempo te quedas?
how long are you staying?

THE TIME

Telling the time in Spanish

In Spanish, the plural is used when telling the time except when it is one o'clock. So to say "it's two o'clock" you would say **son las dos**, and for "it's one o'clock" you would say **es la una**. The 24-hour clock is used in Latin America, for example **son las catorce** (it's two p.m.). Alternatively, you can use the 12-hour clock as in English, clarifying the time of day by adding **de la mañana** (in the morning), **de la tarde** (in the afternoon) or **de la noche** (at night). **De la mañana** is used until midday, **de la tarde** all afternoon and **de la noche** from around sunset onwards.

Some informal expressions
a las dos en punto at 2 o'clock on the dot
son las ocho pasadas it's just past or (Br) gone 8 o'clock
llegar por un pelo to arrive just in time
esperar siglos to wait ages

The basics

half an hour	media hora *med-ya* **aw**-*ra*
in the afternoon	de la tarde *day la* **tar**-*day*
in the evening	por or en or (Arg) a la noche *por/en/a la no-chay*; (before dark) por or en or (Arg) a la tarde *por/en/a la* **tar**-*day*
in the morning	de la mañana *day la man-ya-nah*
midday	mediodía *med-yoh-***dee**-*a*
midnight	medianoche *med-ya-***no**-*chay*
on time	a tiempo *a* **tyem**-*poh*
quarter of an hour	cuarto de hora **kwar**-*toh day* **aw**-*ra*
three quarters of an hour	tres cuartos de hora *tres* **kwar**-*tohs day* **aw**-*ra*
to be early	estar adelantado/a *es-***tar** *a-day-lan-***tah**-*doh/a-day-lan-***tah**-*da*
to be late	estar atrasadao/a *es-***tar** *a-tra-sah-***doh**/a tra-sah-da*

Expressing yourself

what time is it?
¿qué hora es?
kay **aw**-*ra es*

excuse me, do you have the time, please?
perdone, ¿tiene hora?
*pair-***doh**-*nay,* **tyen**-*ay* **aw**-*ra*

it's exactly three o'clock
son las tres en punto
son las trays en **poon**-*toh*

it's nearly one o'clock
es casi la una
es **kas**-*ee la* **oo**-*na*

it's ten past one
es la una y diez
es la oo-na ee dyes

it's half past one
es la una y media
es la oo-na ee med-ya

it's a quarter to one
es la una menos cuarto
es la oo-na may-nos kwar-toh

it's a quarter past one
es la una y cuarto
es la oo-na ee kwar-toh

it's twenty past twelve
son las doce y veinte
son las doh-say ee bayn-tay

it's twenty to twelve
son las doce menos veinte
son las doh-say may-nos bayn-tay

I set my alarm for nine
puse el despertador para las nueve
poo-say el des-pair-ta-dor pa-ra las nway-bay

I arrived at about two o'clock
llegué sobre las dos
yay-gay soh-bray las dos

I got home an hour ago
llegué a casa hace una hora
yay-gay a ka-sa a-say oo-na aw-ra

I waited twenty minutes
esperé veinte minutos
es-pair-ay bayn-tay mee-noo-tohs

the train was fifteen minutes late
el tren llegó con quince minutos de atraso
el trayn yay-goh kon keen-say mee-noo-tohs day a-tras-oh

sorry I'm late
perdón por la demora *or* disculpash, se me hizo tarde
pair-dohn por la day-maw ra/dees-kool-pash, say may ee-so tar-day

let's meet in half an hour
quedemos para dentro de media hora
kay-day-mos pa-ra den-troh day med-ya aw-ra

I'll be back in a quarter of an hour/fifteen minutes
vuelvo dentro de un cuarto de hora/quince minutos
bwel-boh den-troh day oon kwar-toh day aw-ra/keen-say mee-noo-tohs

there's a one-hour time difference between… and…
hay una hora de diferencia entre… y…
eye oo-na aw-ra day dee-fair-en-sya en-tray… ee…

Understanding

sale a las horas y a las medias
departs on the hour and the half-hour

abierto de 10:00 a 16:00
open from 10 a.m. to 4 p.m.

la dan todas las noches a las veintiuna
it's showing every evening at nine

dura una hora y media más o menos
it lasts around an hour and a half

abre a las diez de la mañana
it opens at ten in the morning

por la tarde abre a las cuatro
it opens again at four in the afternoon

NUMBERS

0 cero *say-roh*	**60** sesenta *ses-en-ta*
1 uno *oo-noh*	**70** setenta *set-en-ta*
2 dos *dos*	**80** ochenta *och-en-ta*
3 tres *trays*	**90** noventa *noh-ben-ta*
4 cuatro *kwat-roh*	**100** cien *syen*
5 cinco *seeng-koh*	**101** ciento uno(a) *syen-toh oon-oh*
6 seis *says*	**200** doscientos(as) *dos-syen-tohs*
7 siete *syet ay*	**500** quinientos(as) *keen-yen-tohs*
8 ocho *och-oh*	**1000** mil *meel*
9 nueve *nway-bay*	**2000** dos mil *dos meel*
10 diez *dyes*	**10 000** diez mil *dyes meel*
11 once *on-say*	**1 0000 00** un millón *oon mee-yohn*
12 doce *do-say*	
13 trece *tray-say*	**first** primero *pree-mair-oh*
14 catorce *ka-tor-say*	**second** segundo *se-goon-doh*
15 quince *keen-say*	**third** tercero *tair-sair-oh*
16 dieciséis *dyes-ee-says*	**fourth** cuarto *kwar-toh*
17 diecisiete *dyes-ee-syet-ay*	**fifth** quinto *keen-toh*
18 dieciocho *dyes-ee-och-oh*	**sixth** sexto *sex-toh*
19 diecinueve *dyes-ee-nway-bay*	**seventh** séptimo *sep-tee-moh*
20 veinte *bayn-tay*	**eighth** octavo *ok-tah-boh*
21 veintiuno(a) *bayn-tee-oon-oh*	**ninth** noveno *noh-bay-noh*
22 veintidós *bayn-tee-dos*	**tenth** décimo *des-ee-moh*
30 treinta *trayn-ta*	**twentieth** veinteavo *bayn-tee-ah-boh*
35 treinta y cinco *traynta-ee-seeng-koh*	**twenty-first** veintiunavo *bayn-tee-oon-ah-boh*
40 cuarenta *kwa-ren-ta*	
50 cincuenta *seeng-kwen-ta*	

20 plus 3 equals 23
20 más 3 es igual a 23
bayn-tay mas trays es eeg-wal a bayn-tee-trays

20 minus 3 equals 17
20 menos 3 es igual a 17
bayn-tay may-nos trays es eeg-wal a dyes-ee-syet-ay

20 multiplied by 4 equals 80
20 por 4 es igual a 80
bayn-tay por **kwat**-roh es eeg-**wal** a och-**en**-ta

20 divided by 4 equals 5
20 entre 4 es igual a 5
bayn-tay **en**-tray **kwat**-roh es eeg-**wal** a **seeng**-koh

DICTIONARY

ENGLISH-LATIN AMERICAN SPANISH

A

a un m/una f *(see grammar)*
abbey abadía f
able: to be able to poder
absorbent cotton *(Am)* algodón m (hidrófilo)
about sobre; **to be about to do something** estar a punto de hacer algo
above sobre
abroad en el extranjero or exterior
accept aceptar
access acceso m **74**
accident accidente m **33**, **119**
accommodation alojamiento m
across *(prep)* a través de; **to go across the street** cruzar la calle
adaptor adaptador m
address dirección f **19**, **100**, **101**
admission admisión f
advance: in advance por adelantado **70**
advice consejo m; **to ask someone's advice** pedir consejo a alguien
advise aconsejar
aeroplane *(Br)* avión m
after *(prep)* después de; **after dinner** después de cenar
afternoon tarde f; **in the afternoon** por la tarde
after-sun aftersun® m, loción f post-solar
again otra vez
against contra
age edad f
air aire m
air conditioning aire m acondicionado **41**
airline compañía f aérea
airmail correo m aéreo
airplane *(Am)* avión m
airport aeropuerto m
alarm clock despertador m
alcohol alcohol m
alive vivo
all todo, todos; **all day** todo el día; **all week** toda la semana; **all customers** todos los clientes; **all the time** todo el tiempo; **all inclusive** todo incluido
allergic alérgico **115**, **116**
almost casi
already ya
also también
although aunque
always siempre
ambulance ambulancia f **118**
American *(n)* estadounidense mf, americano m/americana f
American *(adj)* estadounidense, americano; **American plan** *(Am)* pensión f completa
among entre
anaesthetic anestesia f
and y
angry enojado
animal animal m
ankle tobillo m
anniversary aniversario m
another otro
answer *(n)* respuesta f
answer *(v)* responder
answering machine contestador m automático
antibiotics antibiótico m
anybody, anyone *(no matter who)* cualquiera; **do you know anyone?** ¿conoces a alguien?; **I don't know anyone** no conozco a nadie
anything *(no matter what)* cualquier cosa; **do you want anything?** ¿quieres algo?; **I don't have anything** no tengo nada
anyway *(despite that)* de todas formas; *(changing subject)* bueno
apartment apartamento m, departamento m
appendicitis apendicitis f
appointment cita f; **to make an appointment** pedir or hacer una cita; **to have an appointment (with)** tener una cita (con) **112**, **113**

April abril *m*
area zona *f*; **in the area** en la zona; **area code** código *m* de telediscado, *(Mex)* clave *f* LADA **109**
Argentina Argentina *f*
Argentinian *(n)* argentino *m*/argentina *f*
Argentinian *(adj)* argentino
argue pelear(se)
arm brazo *m*
around *(prep)* alrededor de; **around here** por aquí
arrange arreglar; **to arrange to meet** hacer planes para encontrarse, *(Arg)* quedar
arrival llegada *f*
arrive llegar
art arte *m*
artist artista *mf*
as tan; as big/good as... tan bueno/grande como...; **as soon as possible** lo antes posible; **as well as** así como
ashtray cenicero *m* **48**
ask preguntar; **to ask a question** hacer una pregunta
aspirin aspirina *f* **112, 116**
asthma asma *m* **115**
at en; **at the corner** en la esquina
ATM cajero *m* **97**
attack *(v)* atacar, agredir
August agosto *m*
autumn otoño *m*
available *(thing)* disponible; *(person)* libre
avenue avenida *f*
away: 10 kilometres away a 10 kilómetros

B

baby bebé *m*; **baby carriage** *(Am)* cochecito *m* (de bebé); **baby's bottle** biberón *m*
babysitter niñera *f*
back *(part of body)* espalda *f*; **at the back of** detrás de
backpack mochila *f*
bad *(adj)* malo, mal; **it's not bad** no está mal
bag *(plastic)* bolsa *f*; *(handbag)* *(Arg, Peru)* cartera *f*, *(Mex)* bolsa *f*; *(luggage)* maleta *f*, *(Arg)* valija *f*
baggage equipaje *m*; **baggage room** *(Am)* consigna *f*, *(Mex)* guardaequipajes *m*
baker's panadería *f*

balcony balcón *m*
ball pelota *f*, *(Carib)* bola *f*
bandage venda *f*
Band-Aid® *(Am)* curita *f* **112, 116**
bank banco *m* **96**
banknote *(Br)* billete *m*
bar bar *m*
barbecue parrillada *f*, asado *m*
bath baño *m*; **to take a bath** tomar un baño; **bath towel** toalla *f* de baño
bathroom cuarto *m* de baño; *(Am) (toilet)* baño *m*
bathtub *(Am)* bañera *f*
battery *(for torch, radio)* pila *f*; *(for car)* batería **33**
be ser, estar *(see grammar)*
beach playa *f*; **beach umbrella** sombrilla *f*
beard barba *f*
beautiful *(place)* bonito; *(woman)* guapa, *(Arg)* linda, *(Carib)* buena
because porque; **because of** a causa de
bed cama *f*
bee abeja *f*
before *(prep)* antes de; **before dinner** antes de la cena
before *(adv)* antes; **I've seen him before** lo he visto antes
begin empezar
beginner principiante *mf*
beginning principio *m*; **at the beginning** al principio
behind *(prep)* detrás de; **behind the hotel** detrás del hotel
believe creer
below *(adj)* debajo de
beside al lado de
best mejor; **the best** el mejor
better mejor; **to get better** mejorar; **it's better to...** es mejor…
between entre
bicycle bicicleta *f*; **bicycle pump** *(Arg, Peru)* inflador *m* de bicicletas, *(Carib, Mex)* bomba *f* de aire/para bicicletas gomas
big grande
bike bicicleta *f*; **bike path** *(Am)* *(Arg, Peru)* ciclovía *f*, *(Mex)* ruta *f* ciclista **81**
bill *(for electricity)* factura *f*; *(Br)* *(in restaurant)* cuenta *f* **53**; *(Am)* *(note)* billete *m*
bin *(Br)* *(for rubbish)* *(Arg, Peru)* tacho *m*, *(Carib)* zafacón *m*, *(Mex)* bote *m*
binoculars gemelos *mpl*, prismáticos *mpl*
birthday cumpleaños *mpl*
bit pedazo *m*

bite (n) (of dog) mordedura; (of insect) picadura; (snack) algo m de picar
bite (v) morder; (insect) picar 114
black negro
blackout (of lights) apagón m; (fainting) desmayo m
blanket manta f, (Arg, Peru) frazada f, (Mex) cobija f
bleed sangrar
bless: bless you! ¡salud!
blind ciego
blister ampolla f;
blood sangre f; **blood pressure** presión f arterial; **high/low blood pressure** presión f alta/baja
blue azul
boarding embarque m
boat barco m
body cuerpo m
book (n) libro m; **book of tickets** abono m
book (v) reservar 26, 70
bookshop (Br), **bookstore** (Am) librería f
boot bota f; (Br) (of car) (Arg) valijero m, (Carib) baúl m, (Mex) cajuela f, (Peru) maletera f
borrow pedir prestado
both ambos; **both of us** nosotros dos
bottle botella f; **bottle opener** abrebotellas m
bottom (of bag, box) fondo m; **at the bottom (of)** al fondo de
bowl bol m, cuenco m
bra (Arg) soutien m, (Carib) brasiel m, (Mex) brasier m, (Peru) sostén m
brake (n) freno m
brake (v) frenar
bread pan m
break romper; **to break one's leg** romperse una pierna
break down (car) descomponerse, (Carib) quedarse, (Peru) malograrse 33
breakdown (of car) falla f, (Mex) descompostura f; **breakdown service** (Br) servicio m de averías or reparaciones
breakfast desayuno m 40; **to have breakfast** desayunar
bridge puente m
bring traer
brochure folleto m
broken roto
bronchitis bronquitis f
brother hermano m

brown marrón; (hair, eyes) castaño
brush cepillo m
build construir
building edificio m
bump (swelling) (Arg, Carib) chichón m, (Mex) chipote m, (Peru) chinchón m; (in road) bache m, (Carib) hoyo m; (blow) golpe m
bumper parachoques m
buoy boya f
burn (v) quemar; **to burn oneself** quemarse
burst (v) reventar
bus bus m, (Arg, Peru) micro m, (Carib) guagua f, (Mex) camión m 30, 31; **bus route** línea f de bus or (Arg, Peru) micro or (Carib) guagua or (Mex) camión; **bus station** estación f de buses or (Arg, Peru) micros or (Carib) guaguas or (Mex) camiones; **bus stop** parada f de buses or (Arg) micros or (Carib) guaguas or (Mex) camiones, (Peru) paradero m de micros
busy ocupado
but pero
butcher's carnicería f
buy comprar 85
by por; **by car** en coche or (Arg) auto or (Carib, Mex, Peru) carro
bye! ¡adiós!, (Arg) ¡chau!

C

café cafetería f, café m
call (n) llamada f
call (v) llamar 106, 108
call back (call again) llamar otra vez; (return call) devolver la llamada
camera cámara f
camper (person) (Arg) acampante mf, (Mex) campista mf, (Peru) campamentero/a m,f; (Br) (vehicle) casa f (Arg) rodante or (Mex) sobre ruedas, (Carib) caravana f
camping campismo m; **to go camping** ir de camping; **camping stove** cocina f de campamento
campsite camping m 45
can (n) lata f; **can opener** abrelatas m
can (v) (be able) poder; (know how) saber; **I can't open this** no puedo abrir esto; **I can't swim** no sé nadar
Canada Canadá f
Canadian (n) canadiense mf
Canadian (adj) canadiense
cancel cancelar

candle vela *f*
candy *(Am)* caramelo *m; (chocolate)* bombón *m*
car coche *m, (Arg)* auto *m, (Carib, Mex, Peru)* carro *m* **33, 34; car park** *(Br)* estacionamiento *m*, parqueadero *m*
caravan casa *f (Arg)* rodante *or (Mex)* sobre ruedas, *(Carib)* caravana *f*
card tarjeta *f*
carry llevar
case caso *m;* **just in case…** por si acaso, por las dudas
cash dinero *m* efectivo; **to pay cash** pagar en efectivo; **cash desk** *(Br) (in shop)* caja *f*
cashpoint *(Br)* cajero *m* automático **97**
castle castillo *m*
casualty (department) *(Br)* urgencias *fpl*
catch tomar, *(Carib)* coger
cathedral catedral *f*
CD CD *m*
cellphone *(Am)* (teléfono *m*) celular *m* **107**
cemetery cementerio *m*
centimetre centímetro *m*
centre centro *m*
century siglo *m*
chair silla *f*
chairlift telesilla *f*
change *(n)* cambio *m* **86, 87**
change *(v)* cambiar **97**
changing room vestuario *m; (Br) (in shop)* probador *m*
channel canal *m*
chapel capilla *f*
charge *(n) (price)* precio *m;* **bank charges** comisión *f;* **free of charge** gratis; **service charge** servicio *m*
charge *(v) (for product, service)* cobrar
cheap barato
check *(n) (Am)* cheque *m; (restaurant bill)* cuenta *f* **53**
check *(v)* comprobar
check in *(at airport)* registrar
check-in *(at airport)* registro *m* **27**
checkout *(counter)* caja *f*
cheers! *(when drinking)* ¡salud!
chemist's *(Br)* farmacia *f*
cheque *(Br)* cheque *m*
chest pecho *m*
child niño *m*/niña *f*
chimney chimenea *f*
chin barbilla *f*
church iglesia *f*
cigar cigarro *m*, habano *m*

cigarette cigarrillo *m*
cinema *(Br)* cine *m*
circus circo *m*
city ciudad *f;* **city centre** centro *m* (de la ciudad) **41**
clean *(adj)* limpio
clean *(v)* limpiar
cliff acantilado *m*
climate clima *m*
climbing *(sport)* montañismo *m*, andinismo *m*
cloakroom *(Br)* guardarropa *m, (Arg)* ropería *f; (toilet)* baños *mpl*
close *(v)* cerrar
closed cerrado
clothes ropa *f*
clutch *(in car)* embrague *m*
coach bus *m, (Arg)* micro *m, (Mex)* camión *m*, foráneo, *(Per)* bus *m* interprovincial
coast costa *f*
coat saco *m;* **coat check** *(Am)* guardarropa *m, (Arg)* ropería *f*
cockroach cucaracha *f*
coffee café *m*
coil *(contraceptive)* espiral *f*
coin moneda *f*
Coke® Coca-cola®
cold *(n)* resfriado *m, (Arg)* resfrío *m;* **to have a cold** estar resfriado
cold *(adj)* frío; **it's cold** *(weather)* hace frío; **I'm cold** tengo frío
collect call *(Am)* llamada *f* a cobro *or* cargo revertido, *(Mex)* llamada *f* por cobrar **106**
collection *(of stamps, coins)* colección *f; (of mail)* recogida *f*
colour color *m*
comb peine *m*
come venir
come back volver
come in entrar
come out salir
comfortable cómodo
company compañía *f*
compartment compartimento *m*
complain quejarse
complaint queja *f*
comprehensive insurance seguro *m* para *or (Arg)* contra todo riesgo **34**
computer computadora *f*
concert concierto *m* **70; concert hall** sala *f* de conciertos
concession *(Br)* descuento *m* **76**

condom condón m 111
confirm confirmar 28
congratulations! ¡felicidades!,
   ¡felicitaciones!,
connection conexión f 28
constipated estreñido
consulate consulado m
contact (n) contacto m; **contact lenses**
   lentes fpl de contacto
contact (v) contactar 107
contagious contagioso
contraceptive anticonceptivo m
cook (v) cocinar
cooking cocina f; **to do the cooking** hacer
   la comida
cool fresco
corkscrew sacacorchos m
correct (adj) correcto
cost costar; **how much does it cost?**
   ¿cuánto cuesta?
cotton algodón m; **cotton bud** (Br) (Arg,
   Peru) hisopo m (de algodón), (Carib) tip
   m, (Mex) cotonete m; **cotton wool** (Br)
   algodón m (hidrófilo)
couchette (on train) vagón m dormitorio
cough (n) tos f; **to have a cough** tener tos
cough (v) toser
count contar
country (nation) país m; (countryside)
   campo m
course: of course! ¡por supuesto!
cover (n) (on bed) manta f, frazada f, (Mex)
   cobija f
cover (v) cubrir
credit card tarjeta f de crédito 39, 87
cross (n) cruz f
cross (v) cruzar
cruise crucero m
cry llorar
Cuba Cuba f
Cuban (n) cubano m/cubana f
Cuban (adj) cubano
cup taza f
currency moneda f
customs aduana f
cut cortar; **to cut oneself** cortarse
cycle path (Br) (Arg, Peru) ciclovía f, (Mex)
   ruta f ciclista 81

D

damaged dañado; (clothes) estropeado
damp húmedo

dance (v) bailar
dangerous peligroso
dark oscuro; **dark blue** azul oscuro
date (n) fecha f; **out of date** (invalid) (Arg,
   Peru) vencido, (Carib, Mex) caducado;
   date of birth fecha f de nacimiento
date (from) remontarse a
daughter hija f
day día m; **the day after tomorrow**
   pasado mañana; **the day before**
   yesterday anteayer, antes de ayer
dead muerto
deaf sordo
dear (beloved) querido; (expensive) caro
debit card tarjeta f de débito
December diciembre m
declare declarar
deep profundo
degree (temperature) grado m
delay retraso m
delayed retrasado
dentist dentista mf
deodorant desodorante m
department departamento m;
   department store grandes tiendas fpl,
   (Mex) tienda f departamental
departure salida f
depend depender; **that depends (on)**
   depende (de)
deposit depósito m, garantía f, fianza f
dessert postre m 50
develop (photos) revelar 94
diabetes diabetes f
diabetic diabético
dialling code (Br) código m de
   telediscado, (Mex) clave f LADA
diaper (Am) pañal m
diarrhoea diarrea f; **to have diarrhoea**
   tener diarrea
die morir
diesel diesel m
diet dieta f; **to be on a diet** estar a dieta
different (from) diferente de
difficult difícil
digital camera cámara f digital
dinner cena f; **to have dinner** cenar
direct (adj) directo
direction dirección f
directory guía f telefónica; **directory**
   assistance (Am), **directory enquiries** (Br)
   información f telefónica
dirty (adj) sucio
disabled minusválido 74

disaster desastre *m*

disco discoteca *f*

discount descuento *m* 75, 76; **to give someone a discount** hacerle a alguien un descuento

dish plato *m*; **to do the dishes** lavar los platos; **dish of the day** plato del día; **dish towel** paño *m* de cocina

dishwasher lavavajillas *m*

disinfect desinfectar

disposable desechable; **disposable camera** cámara *f* desechable

disturb molestar; **do not disturb** no molestar

dive *(into water)* tirarse al agua; *(underwater)* bucear

diving buceo *m*; **to go diving** bucear

do hacer; **do you have…?** ¿tienes …?

doctor médico *m*/médica *f* 112

dollar dólar *m*

door puerta *f*

downstairs abajo

downtown *(Am)* centro *m* (de la ciudad)

draught beer *(Arg, Peru)* jarra *f*, chop *m*, *(Mex)* shot *m*, *(Carib)* cerveza *f* de barril

dress *(n)* vestido *m*

dress *(v)* vestir; **to get dressed** vestirse

dressing *(bandage)* vendaje *m*; *(for salad)* aliño *m*, condimento *m*, aderezo *m*

drink *(n)* bebida *f*; **to go for a drink** ir a tomar algo *or* un trago 48, 67; **to have a drink** tomar algo *or* un trago

drink *(v)* tomar, beber

drinking water agua *f* potable

drive *(v)* conducir, manejar; **to drive sb** acompañar alguien

driver's license *(Am)*, driving licence *(Br)* carnet *m* de conducir

drops gotas *fpl*

drown ahogarse

drugs *(medicine)* medicamentos *mpl*, medicinas *fpl*, *(Arg)* remedios *mpl*; *(narcotics)* drogas *fpl*

drunk borracho

dry *(adj)* seco; **dry cleaner's** limpieza *f* en seco, *(Arg)* tintorería *f*

dry *(v)* secar

during durante; **during the week** durante la semana

dustbin *(Br)* tacho *m* or *(Mex)* bote *m* de la basura

duty pharmacy farmacia *f* de guardia

each cada; **each one** cada uno

ear oreja *f*

early temprano

earplugs tapones *mpl* para los oídos

earrings *(Arg)* aros *mpl*, *(Carib)* pantallas *fpl*, *(Mex, Peru)* aretes *mpl*

earth tierra *f*

east este *m*; **in the east** en el este; **(to the) east of** (al) este de

Easter Semana *f* Santa, Pascua *f*

easy fácil

eat comer; **to go for something to eat** ir a comer algo 48

economy class clase *f* turista

electric eléctrico; **electric shaver** máquina *f* de afeitar

electricity electricidad *f*; **electricity meter** contador *m* de la luz

elevator *(Am)* ascensor *m*

e-mail *(n)* email *m*, correo *m* electrónico; **e-mail address** (dirección *f* de) email *m*/correo *m* electrónico 103

e-mail: **to email someone** mandar un email a alguien

embassy embajada *f*

emergency urgencia *f*, emergencia *f* 119; **in an emergency** en caso de emergencia; **emergency exit** salida *f* de emergencia; **emergency road service** *(Am)* servicio *m* de averías *or* reparaciones; **emergency room** *(Am)* urgencias *fpl*

empty vacío

end fin *m*, final *m*; **at the end of** al final de

engaged *(to be married)* comprometido; *(Br)* *(phone)* ocupado

engine motor *m*

England Inglaterra *f*

English inglés

Englishman, Englishwoman inglés *m*/inglesa *f*

enjoy disfrutar; **enjoy your meal!** ¡(buen) provecho!; **to enjoy oneself** divertirse

enough bastante, suficiente; **that's enough** es suficiente

enroll inscribirse, anotarse

ensuite bathroom *(Br)* habitación *f* con baño

entrance entrada *f*

entrée entrada *f*

envelope sobre *m*

epileptic epiléptico

equipment equipo *m*

espresso café *m* solo, espresso *m*

Europe Europa *f*

European *(n)* europeo *m*/europea *f*

European *(adj)* europeo

evening noche *f*; *(before dark)* tarde; **in the evening** por *o* en *or (Arg)* a la noche/tarde

every cada; **every day** todos los días

everybody, everyone todo el mundo

everywhere en todas partes

except excepto

exceptional excepcional

excess baggage exceso *m* de equipaje

exchange cambio *m*; **exchange rate** tipo *m* de cambio

excuse *(n)* disculpa *f*

excuse: excuse me perdona

exhausted agotado

exhibit *(Am)*, **exhibition** *(Br)* exposición *f* 75

exit salida *f*

expensive caro

expiry date fecha *f* de expiración *or (Arg, Peru)* vencimiento *or (Mex)* caducidad

express *(adj) (train)* expreso; *(letter)* urgente

extra *(additional charge)* cargo *m* adicional *or* extra

eye ojo *m*

F

face cara *f*

fact hecho *m*; **in fact** en realidad

faint desmayarse

fair *(n)* feria *f*

fall *(v)* caerse; **to fall asleep** dormirse

family familia *f*; **family room** *(Br) (in hotel)* habitación *f* familiar

fan *(hand-held)* abanico *m*; *(electric)* ventilador *m*

far lejos; **far from** lejos de

fare precio *m*

fast rápido, deprisa; **fast food** comida *f* rápida

fat gordo

father padre *m*

faucet *(Am) (Arg)* canilla *f*, *(Carib)* pluma *f*, *(Mex)* llave *f*, *(Peru)* caño *m*

favour favor *m*; **to do someone a favour** hacerle a alguien un favor

favourite favorito

fax fax *m*

February febrero *m*

fed up: to be fed up (with) estar harto (de)

feel sentir; **to feel good/bad** sentirse bien/mal

feeling *(emotional)* sentimiento *m*; *(physical)* sensación *f*

ferry ferry *m*

festival *(celebration)* fiesta *f*; *(for arts)* festival *m*

fetch ir a buscar; **to go and fetch someone/something** ir a buscar a alguien/algo

fever fiebre *f*; **to have a fever** tener fiebre

few pocos

fiancé novio *m*, *(Mex)* prometido *m*

fiancée novia *f*, *(Mex)* prometida *f*

fight lucha *f*

fill llenar

fill in, fill out *(form)* rellenar

fill up rellenar; **to fill up with** *(Am)* **gas** *or (Br)* **petrol** llenar de gasolina *or (Arg)* nafta

filling *(in tooth) (Mex)* resina *f*, *(Peru)* empaste *m*

film *(for camera)* rollo *m* 93, 94; *(movie)* película *f*

finally finalmente

find encontrar

fine *(n)* multa *f*

fine *(adj)* bien; **I'm fine** estoy bien

finger dedo *m*

finish terminar, acabar

fire fuego *m*; **fire brigade** *(Br)*, **fire department** *(Am)* bomberos *mpl*

fireworks fuegos *mpl* artificiales

first primero; **first class** primera clase *f*; **first floor** *(Am)* planta *f* baja; *(Br)* primer piso *m*, primera planta *f*; **first name** nombre *m* (de pila)

fish *(n)* pescado *m*

fishmonger's, fish shop pescadería *f*

fitting room probador *m*

fizzy con gas

flash flash *m*

flask frasco *m*

flat *(adj)* llano, chato; **flat tyre** rueda *f* desinflada

flat *(Br) (n)* apartamento *m*, departamento *m*

flavour sabor *m*, aroma *m*

flight vuelo *m*

flip-flops chancletas *fpl*, *(Arg)* ojotas *fpl*, *(Mex)* huaraches *mpl*, *(Peru)* pantuflas *fpl*

floor *(storey)* piso *m*; *(ground)* suelo *m*

flu gripe *f*

fly *(n)* mosca *f*

fly *(v)* volar

food comida; **food poisoning** intoxicación *f* alimentaria

foot pie *m*; **on foot** caminando

football *(American football)* fútbol *m* americano; *(soccer)* fútbol *m*

for por, para; **for an hour** durante una hora

forbidden prohibido

forehead frente *f*

foreign extranjero

foreigner extranjero *m*/extranjera *f*

forest bosque *m*

fork tenedor *m*

form formulario *m*, *(Mex)* forma *f*

forward *(adv)* hacia adelante

fracture fractura *f*

fragile frágil

free *(at no cost)* gratis; *(at liberty)* libre

freeway *(Am)* autopista *f*, *(Arg, Peru)* carretera *f*

freezer congelador *m*

Friday viernes *m*

fridge *(Br)* *(Arg)* heladera *f*, *(Carib)* nevera *f*, *(Mex)* refrigerador *m*, *(Peru)* refrigeradora *f*

fried frito

friend amigo *m*/amiga *f*

from de, desde; **from... to...** de... a...

front parte *f* delantera; **in front of** delante de

full lleno; **full of** lleno de; **full board** pensión *f* completa; **full price** precio *m* completo

funfair parque *m* de atracciones

fuse fusible *m*

G

gallery galería *f*

game juego *m*

garage *(for parking)* parking *m*, garage *m*; *(for repairs)* taller *m* mecánico

garbage *(Am)* basura *f*; **garbage can** tacho *m* or *(Mex)* bote *m* de la basura

garden jardín *m*

gas gas *m*; *(Am)* *(for car)* gasolina *f*, *(Arg)*

nafta *f* 33; **gas cylinder** *(Arg)* garrafa *f* or *(Carib)* bombona *f* or *(Mex)* tanque *m* or *(Peru)* balón *m* de gas; **gas station** *(Am)*/*(Arg)* estación *f* de servicio, *(Carib)* gasolinera *f*, *(Mex)* gasolinería *f*, *(Peru)* grifo *m*

gate puerta *f*

gay gay *mf*

gearbox caja *f* de cambios

general general

gents' (toilet) *(Br)* baño *m* de caballeros

get *(bus, train)* tomar or *(Carib)* coger

get off *(bus, train)* bajarse de

get up levantarse

girl chica *f*; *(child)* niña *f*

girlfriend novia *f*

give dar

give back devolver

glass *(material)* vidrio *m*; *(container)* vaso *m*; **a glass of water** un vaso de agua

glasses antoojos *mpl*, lentes *mpl*, *(Carib)* espejuelos *mpl*

go ir; **to go to La Habana/to Cuba** ir a La Habana/a Cuba; **we're going home tomorrow** nos vamos a casa mañana

go away irse

go in entrar

go out salir

go out with salir con

golf golf *m*; **golf course** cancha *f* or *(Carib)* campo *m* de golf

good bueno; **good morning** buenos días; **good afternoon** buenas tardes; **good evening** buenas noches

goodbye adiós

goodnight buenas noches *mpl*

GP médico *m*/médica *f* general or de cabecera

grams gramos *mpl*

grass hierba *f*; *(lawn)* césped *m*

great *(excellent)* excelente, estupendo

Great Britain Gran Bretaña *f*

green verde

grey gris

grocer's, grocery store *(Am)* verdulería *f*

ground suelo; **on the ground** en el suelo; **ground floor** *(Br)* planta *f* baja

grow crecer

guarantee garantía *f*

guest huésped *mf*; **guest house** pensión *f*

guide *(person)* guía *mf*; *(book)* guía *f*

guidebook guía *f*

guided tour visita *f* guiada

guy tipo *m*
gynaecologist ginecólogo *m*/ginecóloga *f*

H

hair pelo *m*
hairdresser peluquero *m*/peluquera *f*
hairdrier secador *m* de pelo
half medio; **half a litre/kilo** medio litro/kilo; **half an hour** media hora *f*
half board media pensión *f*
hand mano *f*; **hand baggage** equipaje *m* de mano
handbag *(Arg, Carib, Peru)* cartera *f*, *(Mex)* bolsa *f*
handbrake freno *m* de mano
handkerchief pañuelo *m*
hand-made hecho a mano
hangover resaca *f*
happen pasar, ocurrir
happy feliz
hard duro
hat sombrero *m*
hate odiar
have tener
have to deber, tener que; **I have to go** tengo que irme
hay fever alergia *f* al polen
he él
head cabeza *f*
headache dolor *m* de cabeza; **to have a headache** tener dolor de cabeza
headlight luz *f*, *(Peru)* faro *m*
health salud *f*
hear oir
heart corazón *m*; **heart attack** ataque *m* al corazón
heat calor *m*
heating calefacción *f*
heavy pesado
hello hola
helmet casco *m*
help *(n)* ayuda *f*; **to call for help** pedir ayuda; **help!** ¡socorro! **119**
help *(v)* ayudar **103, 119**
her su; **her car** su coche; **I gave it to her** se lo di a ella; **I talked to her** hablé con ella *(see grammar)*
here aquí; **here is/are** aquí está/están
hers suya, suyo; **it's not my car, it's hers** no es mi coche, es el suyo *(see grammar)*
hi! ¡hola!
high alto; **high school** secundaria *f*,

secundario *m*; **high tide** marea *f* alta
hiking: to go hiking hacer caminata or *(Mex)* senderismo **80**
hill colina *f*
him a él; **I gave it to him** se lo di a él; **I talked to him** hablé con él
himself él mismo
hip cadera *f*
hire *(n)* alquiler *m*
hire *(v)* alquilar
his su; **his car** su coche; **it's not mine, it's his** no es mío, es suyo *(see grammar)*
hitchhike hacer autoestop or *(Arg)* dedo
hitchhiking autoestop *m*
hold sostener
hold on! *(on the phone)* ¡espere!
holiday(s) *(Br)* vacaciones *fpl*; **on holiday** de vacaciones **18**
home casa *f*; **at home** en casa; **to go home** irse a casa
homosexual homosexual *mf*
honest honesto
honeymoon luna *f* de miel, viaje *m* de novios
horse caballo *m*
horseback riding: to go horseback riding *(Am)* andar or montar a caballo, *(Carib)* correr caballo
horse-riding: to go horse-riding *(Br)* andar or montar a caballo, *(Carib)* correr caballo
hospital hospital *m*
hot caliente; **it's hot** hace calor; **hot chocolate** chocolate *m* caliente
hotel hotel *m*
hour hora *f*; **an hour and a half** una hora y media
how cómo; **how are you?** ¿cómo estás?
hungry: to be hungry tener hambre
hurry apuro *m*, *(Carib)* prisa *f*; **to be in a hurry** estar apurado, *(Carib)* tener prisa
hurry (up) darse prisa, apurarse, *(Carib)* avanzar
hurt: it hurts doler; **my foot hurts** me duele el pie
husband marido *m*

I

I yo; **I'm English** soy inglés; **I'm 22 (years old)** tengo 22 años
ice hielo *m*; **ice cube** cubito *m* de hielo

identity card carné m de identidad
identity papers documentos mpl de
　identidad
if si
ill enfermo
illness enfermedad f
important importante
in en; **in England/2007/Spanish** en
　Inglaterra/2007/español; **in an hour**
　dentro de una hora
included incluido
independent independiente
indicator (Br) (in car) intermitente m, (Arg)
　señalero m
infection infección f
information información f **74**
injection inyección f
injured herido
insect insecto m
insecticide insecticida f
inside dentro
instant coffee café m instantáneo
instead en cambio; **instead of** en vez de
instrument (musical) instrumento m
insurance seguro m
intermission (Am) (for play) entreacto m
international internacional; **international
　money order** giro m postal internacional
Internet internet f; **Internet café**
　cibercafé m **102**
interval (Br) (for play) entreacto m
invite invitar
Ireland Irlanda f
Irish irlandés
iron (n) plancha f
iron (v) planchar
island isla f
it ello; **it's beautiful** es precioso; **it's
　warm** hace calor
itchy que pica; **it's itchy** pica
item artículo m

J

jacket chaqueta f, (Arg) campera f, (Mex)
　chamarra f, (Peru) casaca f
January enero m
jetlag jetlag m
jeweller's (Br) joyería f
jewellery joyas fpl
jewelry store (Am) joyería f
job trabajo m
jogging footing m

journey viaje m
jug (Br) jarra f
juice jugo m
July julio m
jumper (Br) suéter m, (Arg) pulóver m,
　(Peru) chompa f
June junio m
just justo; **just before** justo antes; **just a
　little** sólo un poco; **just one** sólo uno;
　I've just arrived acabo de llegar; **just in
　case** por si acaso, por las dudas

K

kayak kayak m
keep mantener
key llave f **41**
kidney riñón m
kill matar
kilometre kilómetro m
kind (sort) tipo m; **what kind of...?** ¿qué
　tipo de ?
kitchen cocina f
knee rodilla f
knife cuchillo m
knock down (by car) atropellar
know (a person) conocer; (a fact) saber;
　I know her la conozco; **I don't know**
　no sé

L

ladies' room (Am), **ladies' (toilet)** (Br)
　baño m de señoras
lake lago m
lamp lámpara f
landscape paisaje m
language lengua f, idioma m
laptop computadora f portátil, laptop f
last (adj) (final) final; (past) pasado; **last
　year** el año pasado
last (v) durar
late tarde **68, 129**
latte café m con leche
laugh (v) reírse
Laundromat®, (Am) **launderette** (Br)
　lavandería f
lawyer abogado m/abogada f
leaflet folleto m
leak (in roof, ceiling) gotera f; (of gas)
　escape m
learn aprender
least: the least menos; **at least** al menos

leave (go out) salir; (go away) irse de
left izquierda f; **to the left (of)** a la izquierda de
left-luggage (office) (Br) consigna f, (Mex) guardaequipajes m
leg pierna f
lend prestar
lens (of glasses) cristal m; (of camera) lente f
lenses (contacts) lentes fpl de contacto
less menos
let (allow) dejar, permitir; (rent out) alquilar
letter carta f
letterbox (Br) buzón m
life vida f
lift (Br) (elevator) ascensor m; **he gave me a lift home** me llevó a casa
light (adj) claro; **light blue** azul claro
light (n) luz f; (lamp) lámpara f; (traffic light) semáforo m; (headlight) faro m, luz f; **do you have a light?** ¿tienes fuego?; **light bulb** (Arg) bombita f, (Carib) bombilla f, (Mex, Peru) foco m
light (v) (cigarette) prender
lighter encendedor m
lighthouse faro m
like (adv) como
like (v) gustar **20**; **I'd like...** me gustaría...
line línea f; (Am) (queue) cola f **77**; **to wait in line** hacer cola
lip labio m
lipstick lápiz m de labios
listen escuchar
listings magazine Guía f del ocio, (Mex) revista f Tiempo libre
litre litro m
little (adj) (small) pequeño, chico; (not much) poco
little (adv) poco
live (v) vivir
liver hígado m
living room sala f, (Arg) living m
local time hora f local
lock (v) cerrar con llave
long largo; **a long time** mucho tiempo; **how long... ?** ¿cuánto tiempo?
look mirar; **you look tired** tienes aspecto cansado
look after cuidar
look at mirar
look for buscar **12, 88**
look like parecerse a
lorry (Br) camión m

lose perder **120**; **to get lost** perderse; **to be lost** estar perdido **13**
lost-and-found (Am), **lost property** (Br) objetos mpl perdidos
lot mucho; **a lot of people** mucha gente; **lots of** muchos
loud alto
love (v) (thing) encantar; (person) querer; **I love dancing** me encanta bailar
low bajo; **low tide** marea f baja
low-fat bajo en grasa
luck suerte f
lucky afortunado; **to be lucky** tener suerte
luggage equipaje m **28**
lunch almuerzo m; **to have lunch** almorzar
lung pulmón m
luxury (n) lujo m
luxury (adj) lujoso

M

magazine revista f
maiden name nombre m de soltera
mail (Am) (n) correo m
mail (Am) (v) mandar por correo
mailbox (Am) buzón m **100**
mailman (Am) cartero m
main principal; **main course** plato m principal
make hacer
mall (Am) centro m comercial, (Arg) shopping m
man hombre m
manage dirigir; **to manage to do something** conseguir hacer algo
manager gerente mf
many muchos; **how many?** ¿cuántos?; **how many times?** ¿cuántas veces?
map mapa m **13, 30, 74**
March marzo m
market mercado m
married casado
mass misa f
match (for fire) fósforo m, (Mex) cerillo m; (game) partido m
material (of clothes) tejido m
matter: it doesn't matter no importa
mattress colchón m
May mayo m
maybe quizás
me me; **she looked at me** me miró; **me too** yo también

meal comida f
mean querer decir; **what does... mean?** ¿qué quiere decir...?; **what does it mean** ¿qué significa?
medicine medicina f
medium (size) mediano; (meat) medio
meet encontrar **68**
meeting reunion f
member miembro m, socio m/socia f
men's room (Am) baño m de caballeros
menu menú m
message mensaje m **107**
meter (gas, electricity) contador m
metre (measure) metro m
Mexican (n) mexicano m/mexicano f
Mexican (adj) mexicano
Mexico (country) México m
Mexico City Ciudad f de México
microwave microondas m
midday mediodía m
middle medio; **in the middle (of)** en medio (de)
midnight medianoche f
might poder; **it might rain** puede ser que llueva
mind: I don't mind no me importa
mine mío, mía (see grammar)
mineral water agua f mineral
minister (in church) pastor m/pastora f
minute minuto m; **at the last minute** en el último minuto
mirror espejo m
Miss Señorita
miss (the train) perder **28**, **31**; **we missed the ferry** perdimos el ferry; **there are two... missing** faltan dos...; **I miss you** te echo de menos, te extraño
mistake error m; **to make a mistake** cometer un error
mobile (phone) (Br) (teléfono m) celular m **107**
modern moderno
modified American plan (Am) media pension f
moisturizer crema f hidratante
moment momento m; **at the moment** en este momento
monastery monasterio m
Monday lunes m
money dinero m, plata f **86**, **97**
month mes m
monument monumento m
mood humor m; **to be in a good/bad**

mood estar de buen/mal humor
moon luna f
moped ciclomotor m
more más; **more than** más que; **much more, a lot more** mucho más; **there's no more...** ya no queda...
morning mañana f
morning-after pill píldora f del día después **116**
mosque mezquita f
mosquito mosquito m
most más: **the most** el más; **el más barato** the cheapest one; **most people** la mayoría de la gente
mother madre f
motorbike (Br), **motorcycle** moto(cicleta) f
motorway (Br) autopista f, (Arg, Peru) carretera f
mountain montaña f; **mountain bike** bicicleta f de montaña; **mountain hut** refugio m de montaña
mouse ratón m
mouth boca f
movie película f; **movie theater** (Am) cine m
Mr Sr.
Mrs Sra.
much mucho; **how much?** ¿cuánto; **how much is it?, how much does it cost?** ¿cuánto es?, ¿cuánto cuesta?
muscle músculo m
museum museo m
music música f **70**
must deber, tener que; **it must be 5 o'clock** deben (de) ser las cinco; **I must go** tengo que irme
my mi (see grammar)
myself yo mismo m/yo misma f

N

nail (of finger) uña f; (metal) clavo m
naked desnudo
name nombre m; **my name is...** me llamo... **15**
nap siesta f; **to take a nap** echar or hacer or dormir una siesta
napkin (for table) servilleta f
nappy (Br) pañal m
narrow angosto
national holiday fiesta f nacional
nature naturaleza f
near cerca; **near the beach** cerca de la

playa; **the nearest…** el… más cercano
necessary necesario
neck cuello *m*
need *(v)* necesitar
neighbour vecino *m*/vecina *f*
neither ni; **neither do I** (ni) yo tampoco;
   neither… nor… ni… ni…
nervous nervioso
never nunca
new nuevo
news noticias *fpl*
newsagent *(shop)* (Arg, Peru) quiosco *m* de
   diarios y revistas, *(Carib, Mex)* puesto *m*
   de periódicos y revistas
newspaper periódico *m*, (Arg, Peru) diario *m*
next *(in time)* siguiente; *(in place)* de al lado
New Year Año *m* Nuevo
nice *(nice-looking)* bonito; *(kind)* simpático
night noche *f* **39, 40**
nightclub discoteca *f*
no no; **no, thank you** no, gracias; **no
   idea** ni idea
nobody nadie
noise ruido *m*; **to make a noise** hacer
   ruido
noisy ruidoso
non-drinking water agua *f* no potable
none ninguno *m*/ninguna *f*
non-smoker no fumador *m*/no fumadora *f*
non-stop sin cesar
noon mediodía *m*
north norte *m*; **in the north** en el norte;
   (to the) north of al norte de
nose nariz *f*
not no; **not yet** aún no; **not at all** *(you're
   welcome)* de nada
note nota *f*
notebook cuaderno *m*
nothing nada
November noviembre *m*
now ahora
nowadays hoy en día
nowhere en ningún sitio
number número *m*
nurse enfermero *m*/enfermera *f*

O

obvious obvio
ocean océano *m*
o'clock en punto; **three o'clock** las tres
   en punto
October octubre *m*

of de
offer *(n)* oferta *f*
often a menudo
oil aceite *m*
ointment pomada *f*
OK *(in agreement)* okey, (Arg) bueno; **are
   you OK?** ¿estás bien?
old antiguo; **how old are you?** ¿cuántos
   años tienes?
on sobre; **on the table** sobre la mesa
once una vez; **once a day/an hour** una
   vez al día/a la hora
one uno *m*/una *f*
one-way ticket *(Am)* (Arg, Peru) pasaje *m*
   de ida, *(Mex)* boleto *m* sencillo
only sólo
open *(adj)* abierto
open *(v)* abrir
operation operación *f*; **to have an
   operation** ser operado
opinion opinión *f*; **in my opinion** en mi
   opinión
opportunity oportunidad *f*
opposite *(n)* contrario *m*/contraria *f*
opposite *(prep)* en frente de
optician's óptica *f*
or o
orange naranja *f*
orchestra orquesta *f*
order *(n)* orden; **out of order** estropeado,
   (Carib) dañado, *(Peru)* malogrado
order *(v)* pedir **50, 51**
organic orgánico
organize organizar
other otro; **others** otros
otherwise *(if not)* si no; *(differently)* de otra
   manera
our nuestro, nuestra, nuestros, nuestras
   (see grammar)
ours nuestro, nuestra *(see grammar)*
outside fuera
oven horno *m*
over encima; **over there** allí
overdone *(food)* demasiado hecho
overweight demasiado pesado; **my
   luggage is overweight** tengo exceso
   de equipaje
owe deber **53, 115**
own *(adj)* propio; **my own car** mi propio
   coche
own *(v)* ser propietario de
owner propietario *m*/propietaria *f*

P

pack empaquetar; **I packed my suitcase** yo me hice la maleta *or* (*Arg*) valija

package paquete *m*

packet paquete *m*

painting cuadro *m*

pair par *m*; **a pair of shorts** un short

palace palacio *m*

panties (*Am*) (*Arg*) bombacha *f*, (*Carib*) panti *m*, (*Mex*) calzones *mpl*, (*Peru*) calzón *m*

pantihose (*Am*) medias *fpl*

pants (*Am*) (*trousers*) pantalón *m*; (*Br*) (*underwear*) (*ladies'*) (*Arg*) bombacha *f*, (*Carib*) panti *m*, (*Mex*) calzones *mpl*, (*Peru*) calzón *m*; (*men's*) calzoncillos *mpl*

paper papel *m*; **paper napkin** servilleta *f* de papel

parcel paquete *m*

pardon? ¿cómo?

parents padres *mpl*

park (*n*) parque *m*

park (*v*) estacionar, parquear, cuadrar

parking lot (*Am*) estacionamiento *m*

parking space estacionamiento *m*, parqueadero *m*

part parte *f*; **to be a part of** ser parte de

party fiesta *f* 71

pass (*n*) (*permit*) pase *m*

pass (*v*) pasar

passenger pasajero *m*/pasajera *f*

passport pasaporte *m*

past pasado; **a quarter past ten** las diez y cuarto

path camino *m*, sendero *m*

patient (*noun*) paciente *mf*

pay pagar 45, 71, 87, 103

pedestrianized street calle *f* peatonal

pee (*v*) hacer pis *or* (*Arg*) pichí *or* (*Mex*) pipí *or* (*Peru*) pila

peel pelar

pen bolígrafo *m*, (*Arg*) lapicera *f*, (*Mex*) pluma *f*, (*Peru*) lapicero *m*

pencil lápiz *m*

people gente *f* 12, 21

percent por ciento

perfect perfecto

perfume perfume *m*

perhaps quizás

period periodo *m*

person persona *f*

personal stereo walkman® *m*

Peru Perú *m*

Peruvian (*n*) peruano *m*/peruana *f*

Peruvian (*adj*) peruano

petrol (*Br*) gasolina *f*, (*Arg*) nafta *f* 33; **petrol station** (*Br*) (*Arg*) estación *f* de servicio, (*Carib*) gasolinera *f*, (*Mex*) gasolinería *f*, (*Peru*) grifo *m*

pharmacy farmácia *f*

phone (*n*) teléfono *m*; **phone booth** cabina *f* (telefónica) 107; **phone call** llamada *f* telefónica; **to make a phone call** hacer una llamada telefónica; **phone number** número *m* de teléfono

phone (*v*) llamar por teléfono, telefonear

phonecard tarjeta *f* telefónica 106

photo foto *f* 93, 94; **to take a photo (of)** sacar *or* tomar una foto (de) 93

picnic picnic *m*; **to have a picnic** hacer un picnic

piece pieza *f*, trozo *m*, pedazo *m*; **a piece of** un trozo de, a piece of fruit una fruta

pill (*contraceptive*) píldora *f*; **to be on the pill** estar tomando la píldora 115

pillow almohada *f*

pillowcase funda *f* de almohada

pimple (*Am*) grano *m*

PIN (number) número *m* personal

pink rosado

pitcher (*Am*) jarra *f*

pity pena *f*; **it's a pity** es una pena

place lugar *m*, sitio *m*

plan plan *m*

plane avión *m* 28

plant planta *f*

plaster (*Br*) (*for cut*) curita *f* 112, 116; **plaster cast** yeso *m*

plastic plástico *m*; **plastic bag** bolsa *f* de plástico

plate plato *m*

platform plataforma *f* 30

play (*n*) (*theatre*) obra *m*

play (*v*) jugar

please por favor

pleased encantado; **pleased to meet you!** ¡encantado de conocerte!

pleasure placer *m*

plug (*in bath*) tapón *m*; (*electrical*) enchufe *m*

plug in enchufar

plumber plomero *m*/plomera *f*, (*Peru*) gasfitero *m*/gasfitera *f*

PO Box casilla *f* de correos

point punto *m*

police policía *f*; **police station** comisaría *f* **119**

policeman policía *m*

policewoman policía *f*

poor pobre

port puerto *m*

portrait retrato *m*

possible posible

post (Br) (n) correo *m*; **post office** (oficina *f* de) correos *mpl* **99**, **100**

post (Br) (v) mandar por correo

postbox (Br) buzón *m* **100**

postcard postal *f*

postcode (Br) código *m* postal

poster póster *m*, cartel *m*

postman (Br) cartero *m*

pot (for cooking) olla *f*; (for plants) maceta *f*

pound libra *f*

powder polvo *m*

practical práctico

pram (Br) cochecito *m* (de bebé)

prefer preferir

pregnant embarazada **115**

prepaid card (for payphone) tarjeta *f* telefónica; (Am) (for cellphone) tarjeta *f* prepago

prepare preparar

present (n) regalo *m* **91**

pressure presión *f*

previous previo

price precio *m*

private privado

prize premio *m*

probably probablemente

problem problema *m*

procession procesión *f*

product producto *m*

profession profesión *f*

programme programa *m*

promise (v) prometer

propose proponer

protect proteger

proud (of) orgulloso (de)

public público; **public holiday** fiesta *f* oficial

pull tirar

purple morado, violeta

purpose propósito *m*; **on purpose** a propósito

purse (Am) (bag) (Arg, Carib, Peru) cartera *f*, (Mex) bolsa *f*; (Br) (wallet) monedero *m*

push empujar

pushchair (Br) sillita *f* (de ruedas),

cochecita *f* (de niños)

put poner

put out (light, fire) apagar

put up (tent) armar

put up with aguantar

Q-Tip® (Am) (Arg, Peru) hisopo *m* (de algodón), (Carib) tip *m*, (Mex) cotonete *m*

quality calidad *f*; **of good/bad quality** de buena/mala calidad

quarter cuarto *m*; **a quarter of an hour** un cuarto de hora; **a quarter to ten** las diez menos cuarto

quay muelle *m*

question pregunta *f*

queue (n) (Br) cola *f*

queue (v) (Br) hacer cola

quick rápido

quickly rápidamente

quiet (calm) tranquilo; (silent) silencioso

quite bastante; **quite a lot of flights** bastantes vuelos

racist racista

racket raqueta *f*

radiator radiador *m*

radio radio *f*; **radio station** emisora *f* (de radio)

railway station (Br) estación *f* de trenes

rain (n) lluvia *f*

rain (v) llover; **it's raining** está lloviendo

raincoat impermeable *m*

random azar *m*; **at random** al azar

rape (v) violar

rare (unusual) raro; (meat) poco hecho

rarely raramente

rather más bien

raw crudo

razor maquinita *f* de afeitar; **razor blade** hoja *f* de afeitar

reach alcanzar

read leer

ready preparado, listo

reasonable razonable

receipt recibo *m* **87**

receive recibir

reception recepción *f*, (Carib) carpeta *f*; **at reception** en la recepción *or* (Carib) carpeta **42**

receptionist recepcionista *mf*

recipe receta *f*

recognize reconocer

recommend recomendar **40**, **48**

red rojo; **to drive through a red light** pasar el semáforo en rojo; **she has red hair** es pelirroja; **red wine** vino *m* tinto

reduce reducir

reduction (in price) rebaja *f*, descuento *m*

refrigerator (Am) (Arg) heladera *f*, (Carib) nevera *f*, (Mex) refrigerador *m*, (Peru) refrigeradora *f*

refund (n) devolución *f* de dinero **90**; **I got a refund** me devolvieron el dinero

refund (v) reembolsar

refuse negarse

register (Am) (in shop) caja *f*

registered (mail) certificado

registration number (número *m* de) matrícula *f*

remember recordar

remind recordar

rent (n) alquiler *m*

rent (v) alquilar **34**, **43**, **80**, **81**

rental alquiler *m*

reopen reabrir, abrir de nuevo

repair reparar, arreglar **34**

repeat repetir

reserve reservar **26**, **40**, **42**, **45**, **49**

reserved reservado

rest: the rest resto *m*

rest (v) descansar

restaurant restaurante *m* **48**

restrooms (Am) baños *mpl* **8**

return (n) vuelta *f*; **return ticket** (Br) boleto *m* or (Arg) pasaje *m* de ida y vuelta

reverse-charge call (Br) llamada *f* a cobro or cargo revertido, (Mex) llamada *f* por cobrar **106**

reverse gear marcha *f* atrás

rheumatism reuma *f*

rib costilla *f*

right (n) (not left) derecha *f*; (entitlement) derecho; **to the right (of)** a la derecha (de); **to have the right to…** tener derecho a…

right (adj) (not left) derecho; (correct) correcto; **all right** de acuerdo; **are you all right?** ¿estás bien?

right (adv) justo; **right away** enseguida; **right beside** justo al lado

ring (v) (on phone) llamar

ripe maduro

rip-off robo *m*, engaño *m*

risk (v) arriesgar

river río *m*

road carretera *f*; **road sign** señal *f* de tráfico

rock piedra *f*, roca *f*

rollerblades patines *mpl* en línea

room cuarto *m*; (in hotel) habitación *f* **39**, **40**, **41**

rosé wine vino *m* rosado

round (adj) redondo

roundabout (Br) rotonda *f*

round-trip ticket (Am) boleto *m* or (Arg) pasaje *m* de ida y vuelta

rubbing alcohol (Am) alcohol *m*

rubbish (Br) basura *f*

rucksack mochila *f*

rug alfombra *f*

ruins ruinas *fpl*; **in ruins** en ruinas

run correr

run out (come to an end) agotarse

S

sad triste

safe seguro

safety seguridad *f*

sail (v) navegar

sailing navegación *f*; **to go sailing** salir a navegar

sale venta *f*; (low prices) liquidación *f*, ofertas *fpl*; **for sale** en venta; **in the sale** en liquidación, en oferta

sales liquidación *f*, rebajas *fpl*, ofertas *fpl*

sales assistant vendedor *m*, vendora *f*

salt sal *f*

salty salado

same mismo *m*/misma *f*; **the same** el mismo **52**

sand arena *f*

sandals sandalias *fpl*

sanitary napkin (Am), **sanitary towel** (Br) toalla *f* sanitaria or higiénica

Saturday sábado *m*

save (v) (money) ahorrar; (rescue) salvar

say decir; **how do you say… ?** ¿cómo se dice…?

scared asustado; **to be scared (of)** tener miedo (de/a)

scenery paisaje *m*

scissors tijeras *fpl*

scoop (of ice cream) bola *f*

scooter (motorcycle) Vespa® f
scotch (whisky) whisky m escocés
Scotch tape® (Am) cinta f Scotch®
Scotland Escocia f
Scottish escocés
scuba diving buceo m
sea mar m
seafood marisco m
seasick mareado
seaside playa f; **at the seaside** en la playa
season temporada f
seat asiento m **26**
seatbelt cinturón m de seguridad
sea view vista f al mar
second segundo; **second class** segunda clase f
secondary school (Br) secundaria f, secundario m
second-hand de segunda mano
secure seguro
security seguridad f
see ver; **see you later!** ¡hasta luego!; **see you tomorrow!** ¡hasta mañana!
seem parecer; **it seems that…** parece que…
self-catering (Br) con cocina propia
sell vender **85**
Sellotape® (Br) cinta f Scotch®
send enviar
sender remitente mf
sense sentido m
sensitive sensible
sentence frase f
separate (v) separar
separately por separado
September septiembre m
serious (person) serio; (illness) grave
several varios
sex sexo m
shade sombra; **in the shade** a la sombra
shame (disgrace) vergüenza f; (pity) pena f, lástima f; **what a shame!** ¡que pena or lástima!
shampoo champú m
shape forma f
share (v) compartir
shave afeitarse
shaver maquinita f eléctrica
shaving cream crema f de afeitar
shaving foam espuma f de afeitar
she ella
sheet sábana f
shellfish marisco m

shirt camisa f
shock (jolt) choque m; (surprise) shock m
shocking (surprising) chocante
shoes zapatos mpl
shop (Br) tienda f; **shop assistant** vendedor m/vendedora f
shopkeeper (Br) tendero m/tendera f
shopping compras fpl; **to do the shopping** ir de compras, (Carib) hacer compra; **shopping cart** (Am) carrito m; **shopping centre** (Br) centro m comercial, (Arg) shopping m
short corto; **I'm two… short** me hacen falta dos…; **short cut** atajo m
shorts pantalón m corto, short m
shoulder hombro m
show (n) espectáculo m **70**
show (v) mostrar
shower ducha f; **to take a shower** ducharse; **shower gel** gel m de baño
shut (v) cerrar
shuttle (bus) camioneta f, van f (Peru) custer m
shy tímido
sick (unwell) enfermo; **to feel sick** (nauseous) tener ganas de vomitar
side lado m
sign (n) señal f
sign (v) (letter, form) firmar
signal señal f
silence silencio m
silver plata f
simple sencillo, simple
since desde
sing cantar
singer cantante mf
single (person) soltero; (room) individual; **single ticket** (Br) (Arg, Peru) pasaje m de ida, (Mex) boleto m sencillo
sister hermana f
sit down sentarse
size tamaño m; (of garment) talla f, (Arg) talle m **90**; (of shoes) número m **90**; (of person) estatura f
ski (v) esquiar; **ski boots** botas fpl de esquí; **ski lift** telesquí m; **ski pole** or (Br) **stick** bastón m; **ski resort** estación f de esquí
skiing esquí m; **to go skiing** esquiar
skin piel f
skirt falda f
sky cielo m
skyscraper rascacielos m

sleep (n) sueño m
sleep (v) dormir; **to sleep with** dormir con
sleeping bag saco m de dormir
sleeping car (on train) vagón m dormitorio
sleeping pill somnífero m
sleeve manga f
slice (of bread) rebanada f; (of ham) loncha f, (Arg) feta f; (of cake) trozo m
sliced cortado en rebanadas
slow lento
slowly lentamente, despacio
small pequeño
smell (n) olor m
smell (v) oler; **to smell good/bad** oler bien/mal
smile (v) sonreír
smoke (n) humo m
smoke (v) fumar
smoker fumador m/fumadora f
snack aperitivo m, (Arg) merienda f, (Peru) piqueo m
snow (n) nieve f
snow (v) nevar; **it's snowing** nieve
so así que; **so that** para que
soap jabón m
soccer fútbol m
socks medias fpl, (Mex) calcetines mpl
some algún m/alguna f; **some tourists** algunos turistas
somebody, someone alguien
something algo; **something else** algo más
sometimes a veces
somewhere en algún sitio; **somewhere else** en otro sitio
son hijo m
song canción f
soon pronto
sore dolorido, inflamado; **to have a sore throat** tener dolor de garganta, tener la garganta inflamada
sorry! ¡lo siento!, ¡perdón!
south sur m; **in the south** en el sur; **(to the) south of** (al) sur de
souvenir recuerdo m
Spain España f
Spanish español m/española f
spare tyre, spare wheel rueda f (Arg) auxiliar or (Mex) de repuesto, (Carib) respuesta f **33**
speak hablar **8, 10, 119**
special (n) especialidad f; **today's special** plato m del día **50**

specialty (Am), **speciality** (Br) especialidad f
speed velocidad f
spell deletrear; **how do you spell it?** ¿cómo se escribe?
spend gastar
spice especia f
spicy picante
spider araña f
splinter astilla f
split up separarse
spoil estropear
sponge esponja f
spoon cuchara f
sport deporte m
sporty deportivo
spot (place) sitio m; (Br) (pimple) grano m
sprain torcerse; **to sprain one's ankle** torcerse el tobillo
spring primavera f
square (n) (in town) plaza f; (shape) cuadrado m
stadium estadio m
stain mancha f
stained-glass window vitral m
stairs escaleras fpl
stamp sello m, estampilla f **100**
start (v) empezar
starter (Br) entrada f
state estado m
statement declaración f
station estación f
stay (n) estadía f
stay (v) quedarse; **to stay in touch** seguir en contacto
steal robar **119, 121**
step paso m
still (adv) todavía
still water (Br) agua m sin gas
sting (n) (by insect) picadura f; (burning) ardor m
sting (v) (insect) picar **114**; (burn) arder
stock existencias fpl; **out of stock** agotado
stomach estómago m
stone (rock) piedra f; (in fruit) (Arg) carozo m, (Carib) pepita f, (Mex) hueso m, (Peru) pepa f
stop (n) parada f, (Peru) paradero m **31**
stop (v) parar
store (Am) tienda f
storey piso m
storm tormenta f

straight ahead, straight on todo recto
strange extraño
street calle f
streetcar (Am) tranvía m
stroller (Am) sillita f (de ruedas), cochecito m (de niños)
strong fuerte
stuck atascado, (Am) tapado, (Peru) atorado
student estudiante mf
study estudiar **16**
style estilo m
subtitled subtitulado
suburb barrio m periférico
subway (Am) metro m, (Arg) subte m **30**; **subway station** (Am) estación f de metro or (Arg) subte
suffer sufrir
suggest sugerir
suit convenir; **does that suit you?** ¿te viene bien?
suitcase maleta f, (Arg) valija f
summer verano m
summit cima f
sun sol m; **in the sun** al sol; **sun cream** bronceador m
sunbathe tomar el sol
sunburnt quemadura f (de sol); **to get sunburnt** quemarse
Sunday domingo m
sunglasses gafas fpl or anteojos mpl or lentes mpl de sol
sunhat sombrero m
sunrise amanecer m
sunset anochecer m
sunstroke insolación f; **to get sunstroke** tener una insolación
supermarket supermercado m **44**, **85**
supplement suplemento m
sure seguro
surf (v) surfear, hacer surf
surfboard tabla f de surf
surfing surfing m; **to go surfing** surfear, hacer surf
surgical spirit (Br) alcohol m
surname apellido m
surprise (n) sorpresa f
surprise (v) sorprender
sweat (v) sudar
sweater suéter m, (Arg) pulóver m, (Peru) chompa f
sweet (Br) (n) caramelo m; (chocolate) bombón m

sweet (adj) dulce
swim (v) nadar
swimming natación m; **swimming pool** piscina f **44**, **82**; **swimming trunks** traje m or (Peru) ropa f de baño
swimsuit traje m de baño
switch off apagar
switch on encender
swollen hinchado
synagogue sinagoga f
syrup jarabe m

T

table mesa f **49**
tablespoon cuchara f de servir
tablet pastilla f
take tomar; **it takes 2 hours** demora or lleva 2 horas
take off (plane) despegar
takeaway (Br), **takeout** (Am) comida f para llevar
talk hablar
tall alto
tampon tampón m **112**
tan (n) bronceado m
tan (v) broncearse
tanned bronceado
tap (Br) (Arg) canilla f, (Carib) pluma f, (Mex) llave f, (Peru) caño m
taste (n) sabor m
taste (v) saber; **to taste good** saber bien
tax impuesto m
tax-free libre de impuestos
taxi taxi m **34**; **taxi driver** taxista mf
team equipo m
teaspoon cucharita f
teenager adolescente mf
telephone (n) teléfono m
telephone (v) llamar por teléfono, telefonear
television televisión f
tell decir
temperature temperatura f; **to have a temperature** tener fiebre **114**; **to take one's temperature** tomarse la fiebre
temple templo m
temporary temporal
tennis tenis m; **tennis court** cancha f de tenis
tent (Arg, Peru) carpa f, (Carib) caseta f, (Mex) tienda f
terminal terminal f

terrace terraza f
terrible terrible
thanks gracias fpl; **thanks to** gracias a
thank you gracias; **thank you very much**
  muchas gracias
that aquel, aquella; **that one** aquél,
  aquélla
the el m/la f (see grammar)
theatre teatro m
theft robo m
their su, sus; **their room** su cuarto; **their**
  passports sus pasaportes (see grammar)
theirs suyo, suya, suyos, suyas (see
  grammar)
them los, las, les (see grammar)
theme park parque m temático
then entonces
there allí; **there is, there are** hay
therefore por tanto
thermometer termómetro m
these estos mpl, estas fpl; **these ones**
  éstos, éstas
they ellos mpl, ellas fpl; **they say that...**
  dicen que... (see grammar)
thief ladrón m/ladrona f
thin delgado
thing cosa f
think pensar; **to think about...** pensar
  en...
thirsty: to be thirsty tener sed
this este m, esta f; **this one** éste, ésta;
  this evening esta tarde; **this is my**
  husband éste es mi marido
those aquellos mpl, aquellas fpl; **those**
  ones aquéllos mpl/aquéllas fpl
throat garganta f
throw tirar
throw out (rubbish) tirar, arrojar; (person)
  echar
Thursday jueves m
ticket (for travel) boleto m, (Arg) pasaje m
  26; (for show) entrada f **69**, **70**; **ticket**
  office boletería f; (at theatre etc) taquilla f
tidy ordenado
tie (n) corbata f
tie (v) atar
tight apretado
tights (Br) medias fpl
time tiempo m; hora f; **what time is it?**
  ¿qué hora es?; **from time to time**
  de vez en cuando; **on time** puntual;
  three/four times tres/cuatro veces;
  time difference diferencia f horaria

timetable horario m **26**
tip propina f
tired cansado
tiring cansador
tobacconist's tabaquería f
today hoy
together juntos
toilet baño m; **toilets** (Br) baños mpl **8**;
  toilet paper papel m higiénico or (Carib)
  de inodoro or (Mex) de baño
toiletries artículos mpl de tocador or
  personales or de aseo personal
toll peaje m
tomorrow mañana; **tomorrow evening**
  mañana por or en or (Arg) a la tarde;
  tomorrow morning mañana por or en
  or (Arg) a la mañana
tongue lengua f
tonight esta noche
too (also) también; (excessively) demasiado;
  too many demasiados; **too much**
  demasiado
tooth diente m
toothbrush cepillo m de dientes
toothpaste pasta f de dientes
top (upper part) parte f superior; **at the top**
  en la parte superior
top-up card (Br) (for mobile phone) tarjeta
  f prepago
torch linterna f
touch tocar
tourist turista mf; **tourist office** oficina f
  de turismo **74**
towards hacia
towel toalla f
town ciudad f; **town centre** (Br) centro m
  (de la ciudad); **town hall** municipalidad
  f, (Carib) alcaldía f
toy juguete m
traditional tradicional
traffic tráfico m; **traffic circle** (Am) rotonda
  f; **traffic jam** (Arg) embotellamiento m,
  (Mex) tapón m, (Peru) atolladero m **33**
trailer (Am) casa f (Arg) rodante or (Mex)
  sobre ruedas, (Carib) caravana f
train tren m **30**, **31**; **the train to...** el tren
  a ...; **train station** estación f de tren
tram (Br) tranvía m
transfer (of money) transferencia f, (Arg,
  Peru) giro m
translate traducir
travel viajar; **travel agency** agencia f
  de viajes

traveller's cheque cheque *m* de viaje
trip viaje; **have a good trip!** ¡buen viaje!
trolley *(Br)* carrito *m*
trouble problema *m*; **to have trouble
    doing something** tener problemas para
    hacer algo
trousers *(Br)* pantalón *m*
truck camión *m*
true verdadero; **it's true** es verdad
trunk *(Am) (of car) (Arg)* valijero *m*, *(Carib)*
    baúl *m*, *(Mex)* cajuela *f*, *(Peru)* maletera *f*
try intentar; **to try to do something**
    intentar hacer algo
try on probarse **90**
Tuesday martes *m*
turn *(n)* turno *m*; **it's your turn** te toca
turn *(v)* girar, **turn signal** *(Am)* intermitente
    m, *(Arg)* señalero *m*
twice dos veces
type *(n)* tipo *m*
type *(v)* escribir a máquina
typical típico
tyre neumático *m*, *(Arg)* goma *f*

umbrella paraguas *m*
uncle tío *m*
uncomfortable incómodo
under debajo de
underground *(Br) (train)* metro *m*, *(Arg)*
    subte *m* **30**; **underground station** *(Br)*
    estación *f* de metro *or (Arg)* subte
underneath *(prep)* debajo de
underpants *(for men)* calzoncillos *mpl*
understand entender, comprender **10**
underwear ropa *f* interior
United Kingdom Reino Unido *m*
United States Estados Unidos *mpl*
until hasta
upset *(adj) (displeased)* disgustado; **to
    have an upset stomach** estar mal del
    estómago
upstairs arriba
urgent urgente
us nos, a nosotros *(see grammar)*
use usar; **to be used for** usarse para; **I'm
    used to it** estoy acostumbrado
useful útil
useless inútil
usually normalmente
U-turn *(on road)* cambio *m* de sentido

vacation *(Am)* vacaciones *fpl*; **on vacation**
    de vacaciones **18**
vaccinated (against) vacunado (contra)
valid (for) válido (para)
valley valle *m*
VAT IVA *m*
vegetarian vegetariano **60**
very muy
view vista *f*
villa *(in country)* casa *f* de campo; *(chalet)*
    chalet *m*
village pueblo *m*
visa *(permit)* visa *f*
visit *(n)* visita *f*
visit *(v)* visitar
volleyball vóleibol *m*
vomit *(v)* vomitar

waist cintura *f*
wait esperar; **to wait for something/
    someone** esperar algo/a alguien
waiter *(Mex, Carib)* camarero *m*, mesero
    m, *(Arg, Peru)* mozo *m*
waitress camarera *f*
wake up despertar(se)
Wales (País de) Gales *m*
walk *(n)* paseo *m* **80**; **to go for a walk** dar
    un paseo
walk *(v)* caminar
walking: **to go walking** hacer caminatas
    or (Mex) senderismo; **walking boots**
    botas *fpl* de caminar
wallet *(Arg, Peru)* billetera *f*, *(Mex)* cartera *f*
want querer; **to want to do something**
    querer hacer algo
warm caliente; **it's very warm** *(weather)*
    hace mucho calor
warn advertir
wash *(n)* lavado *m*; **to have a wash** lavarse
wash *(v)* lavar; **to wash one's hair** lavarse
    el pelo
washbasin *(Arg)* pileta *f*, *(Carib)* lavamanos
    m, *(Mex)* lavabo *m*, *(Peru)* lavatorio *m*
washing *(of clothes)* lavado *m*; **to do
    the washing** lavar la ropa; **washing
    machine** lavadora *f*; **washing powder**
    detergente *m*; **washing-up liquid**
    (detergente *m*) lavavajillas *m*

wasp avispa f
waste malgastar
watch (n) reloj m
watch (v) mirar; watch out! ¡cuidado!
water agua f 51, 52
waterproof impermeable
waterskiing esquí m acuático
wave (n) ola f
way (method) manera f; (route) camino m;
 way in entrada f; way out salida f
we nosotros, nosotras (see grammar)
weak débil
wear (clothes) llevar, vestir
weather tiempo m 22, 23; the weather's
 bad hace mal tiempo; weather forecast
 pronóstico m del tiempo 22
website sitio m web, website f
Wednesday miércoles m
week semana f
weekend fin m de semana
welcome bienvenido; you're welcome
 de nada
well bien; I'm very well estoy muy bien;
 well done (meat) bien hecho or (Arg)
 corcido
well-known muy conocido
Welsh galés m/galesa f
west oeste m; in the west en el oeste; (to
 the) west of (al) oeste de
wet mojado; (slightly) húmedo
wetsuit traje m isotérmico
what qué; what do you want? ¿qué
 quiere?
wheel rueda f
wheelchair silla f de ruedas
when cuándo
where dónde; where is/are...? ¿dónde
 esta/están?; where are you from? ¿de
 dónde eres?; where are you going?
 ¿dónde vas?
which cuál
while mientras
white blanco; white wine vino m blanco
who quién; who's calling? ¿de parte de
 quién?
whole entero; the whole cake todo el
 pastel
whose cuyo m/cuya f
why por qué
wide ancho
wife mujer f, esposa f
wild (animal) salvaje; (plant) silvestre

wind viento m
window ventana f; (of shop) vitrina f, (Arg)
 vidriera f
windscreen (Br), windshield (Am)
 parabrisas m
windsurfing windsurf(ing) m
wine vino m 51
winter invierno m
with con
withdraw retirar
withdrawal retiro
without sin
woman mujer f
wonderful maravilloso
wood (material) madera f; (forest) bosque m
wool lana f
work (n) trabajo m
work (v) (in job) trabajar 16; (function)
 funcionar, andar 41, 103
world mundo m
worse peor; to get worse empeorar; it's
 worse (than) es peor (que)
worth: to be worth 50 pesos valer 50
 pesos; it's worth it vale la pena
wound herida f
wrist muñeca f
write escribir 11
wrong equivocado; you're wrong estás
 equivocado

XYZ

X-ray (picture) radiografía f

year año m
yellow amarillo
yes sí
yesterday ayer; yesterday evening ayer
 por la tarde
you tú; vos; usted; ustedes (see grammar)
young joven
your tu, (Arg) vos; su (see grammar)
yours tuyo, tuya, tuyos, tuyas; su, sus
 (see grammar)
youth hostel albergue m juvenil

zero cero
zip (Br) cierre m, (Carib) zip m
zip code (Am) código m postal
zipper (Am) cierre m, (Carib) zip m
zoo zoo m, zoológico m
zoom (lens) zoom m, teleobjetivo m

DICTIONARY

LATIN AMERICAN SPANISH-ENGLISH

A

a to
abadía f abbey
abajo downstairs
abanico m fan
abeja f bee
abierto open
abogado m, **abogada** f lawyer
abolladura bump
abrebotellas m bottle opener
abrelatas m can opener
abril m April
abrir to open
acá here; **acá está/están** here is/are
acabar to finish, to end; **acabar de...** to have just...
acantilado m cliff
acaso: por si acaso just in case
acceso m access
accidente m accident
aceite m oil
aceptar to accept
aconsejar to advise
acostumbrado accustomed, used
acuerdo: de acuerdo in agreement; all right
adaptador m adaptor
adelantado: por adelantado in advance
aderezo m salad dressing
¡adiós! bye!
admisión f admission
adolescente mf teenager
aduana f customs
advertir to warn
aeropuerto m airport
afeitarse to shave, to have a shave
afortunado lucky; **tener suerte** to be lucky
agarrar to catch, to take, to get
agencia f **de viajes** travel agency
agosto m August
agotado exhausted; out of stock
agotarse to run out

agredir to attack
agua m water; **agua con gas** sparkling water; **agua mineral** mineral water; **agua no potable** non-drinking water; **agua potable** drinking water; **agua sin gas** still water
aguantar to put up with, to stand
agujero m hole
ahogarse to drown
ahora now
ahorrar to save
aire m air; **aire acondicionado** air conditioning
al to the; **al cine** to the (Am) movie theater or (Br) cinema
alberca f swimming pool
albergue m **juvenil** youth hostel
alcaldía f town hall
alcanzar to reach
alcohol m alcohol; (Am) rubbing alcohol, (Br) surgical spirit
alergia f allergy; **alergia al pollen** hay fever
alérgico allergic
alfombra f rug, mat
algo something; **algo más** something else
algodón m cotton; **algodón hidrófilo** (Am) absorbent cotton, (Br) cotton wool
alguien somebody, someone
algún m, **alguna** f some; **algunos turistas** some tourists
aliño m salad dressing
allá, allí there
almacén (Am) store, (Br) shop
almohada f pillow
almorzar to have lunch
almuerzo m lunch
alojamiento m accommodation
alpinismo m climbing
alquilar to let, to rent, to hire
alquiler m rent, hire, rental
alrededor de around
alto high, tall; loud
amanecer m sunrise, dawn

amarillo yellow
ambos both
ambulancia f ambulance
americano American
americano m, **americana** f American
amigo m, **amiga** f friend
ampolla f blister
ancho wide
anciano m, **anciana** f old man, old woman
andar to walk
andinismo m climbing
anestesia f anaesthetic
angosto narrow
animal m animal
aniversario m anniversary
anochecer m sunset, nightfall
anotarse to enrol, to sign up
anteayer the day before yesterday
antelación: con antelación in advance
antes before
antibióticos mpl antibiotics
anticonceptivo m contraceptive
año m year; **Año Nuevo** New Year;
  ¿cuántos años tienes? how old are you?
apagar to turn out, to switch off; to put
  out, to extinguish
apagón m power cut, blackout
aparcamiento m parking space; (Am)
  parking lot, (Br) car park
aparcar to park
apartamento m apartment
apellido m surname
apendicitis f appendicitis
aprender to learn
apretado tight
aprovechar: ¡que aproveche! enjoy your
  meal!
apuro m hurry; **tener apuro** to be in a
  hurry
aquel m, **aquella** f that; that one
aquellos mpl, **aquellas** fpl those; those
  ones
aquí here; **aquí está/están** here is/are
araña f spider
arder to sting, to burn
ardor m sting, burning sensation
arena f sand
aretes mpl earrings
Argentina f Argentina
argentino Argentinian
argentino m, **argentina** f Argentinian
armar to put up (tent)
aros mpl earrings

arreglar to arrange; to repair
arriba up, upstairs
arriesgar to risk
arrojar to throw
arte m art
artículo m item, article; **artículos de aseo**
  or **de tocador** toiletries
artista mf artist
asado m barbecue
ascensor m (Am) elevator, (Br) lift
así like this, like that; **así que** so; **así como**
  as well as
asiento m seat
asma f asthma
aspirina f aspirin
astilla f splinter
asustado scared, frightened
atacar to attack
atajo m short cut
ataque m **al corazón** heart attack
atar to tie
atascado stuck, jammed; blocked
atorado stuck, jammed; blocked
atrasado delayed
atraso m delay
atropellar to knock down
aún still, yet
aunque although
autoestop m hitchhiking; **hacer autoestop**
  to hitchhike
autopista f (Am) freeway, (Br) motorway
avenida f avenue
avería breakdown; **tener una avería** to
  break down
averiado out of order
avión m plane
avispa f wasp
ayer yesterday; **ayer por la tarde**
  yesterday evening
ayuda f help; **pedir ayuda** to call for help
ayudar to help
azar m random; **al azar** at random
azul blue

B

bache m hole in the road
bailar to dance
bajarse de to get off, get out
bajo under; low; **bajo en grasa** low-fat
balcón m balcony
balón m ball
balde m bin; **balde de la basura** (Am)

garbage can, *(Br)* dustbin
banco *m* bank
bañera *f* bathtub
baño *m* toilet; swim; **baño de hombres** or **caballeros** *(Am)* men's room, *(Br)* gents' toilet; **baño de damas** or **señoras** *(Am)* ladies' room, *(Br)* ladies' toilet; **darse un baño** to go for a swim; **tomar un baño** to take a bath
baños *mpl (Am)* restrooms, *(Br)* toilets
bar *m* bar
barato cheap
barba *f* beard
barbacoa *f* barbecue
bárbaro great
barbilla *f* chin
barco *m* boat
barrio *m* **periférico** suburb
bastante enough; quite; **¿tienes bastante?** do you have enough?; **bastantes vuelos** quite a lot of flights
bastón *m* ski pole, *(Br)* ski stick
bastoncillo *m* **(de algodón)** *(Am)* Q-Tip®, *(Br)* cotton bud
basura *f (Am)* garbage, *(Br)* rubbish
batería *f* battery
baúl *m (Am)* trunk, *(Br)* boot *(of car)*
bebé *m* baby
beber to drink
bebida *f* drink
biberón *m* baby's bottle
biblioteca *f* library
bici *f* bike
bicicleta *f* bicycle; **bicicleta de montaña** mountain bike
bien well, all right, fine; **¿estás bien?** are you all right?; **estoy bien** I'm fine; **estoy muy bien** I'm very well; **bien hecho** or **cocido** well done *(meat)*
bienvenido welcome
billete *m* ticket; *(Am)* bill, *(Br)* banknote; **billete de ida** one-way ticket, *(Br)* single ticket; **billete de ida y vuelta** *(Am)* round-trip ticket, *(Br)* return ticket
billetera *f* wallet
blanco white; **vino blanco** white wine
boca *f* mouth
bol *m* bowl
bola *f* ball; scoop
boleta *f* receipt
boletería *f* ticket office
boleto *m* ticket; **boleto de ida** *(Am)* one-way ticket, *(Br)* single ticket; **boleto de**

ida y vuelta *(Am)* round-trip ticket, *(Br)* return ticket
bolígrafo *m* ballpoint pen
bolsa *f* bag; *(Am)* purse, *(Br)* handbag; **bolsa de plástico** plastic bag
bolso *m* bag
bomba de gasolina *f (Am)* gas station, *(Br)* petrol station
bombachas *fpl Am* panties, *(Br)* pants, knickers
bomberos *mpl (Am)* fire department, *(Br)* fire brigade
bombilla *f* light bulb
bombón *m* chocolate
bombona *f* **de butano** gas cylinder
borracho drunk
bosque *m* wood, forest
bota *f* boot, **botas de caminar** walking boots; **botas de esquí** ski boots
botella *f* bottle
boya *f* buoy
brazier *m* bra
brazo *m* arm
brevet *m (Am)* driver's license, *(Br)* driving licence
bronceado tanned, suntanned, brown
bronceado *m* tan, suntan
bronquitis *f* bronchitis
bucear to dive
buceo *m* diving; **bucear** to go diving
buen(o) good; **buen(os) día(s)** good morning; **buenas noches** good evening, good night; **buenas tardes** good afternoon
bus *m* bus
buscar to look for, to search for
buzón *m (Am)* mailbox, *(Br)* postbox

C

caballo *m* horse; **andar** or **montar a caballo, correr caballo** to go *(Am)* horseback riding or *(Br)* horse-riding
cabeza *f* head
cabina *f* **(telefónica)** phone booth
cada each, every; **cada uno** each one
cadera *f* hip
caducado out of date
caer(se) to fall
café *m* café, cafeteria; coffee; **café con leche** coffee with milk; **café instantáneo** instant coffee; **café solo** espresso
cafetería *f* café, cafeteria

caja f (in supermarket) checkout; (in smaller shop) (Am) register, (Br) cash desk; (container) box; **caja de ahorros** savings bank; **caja de cambios** gearbox

cajero m **(automático)** ATM, (Br) cashpoint

calcetines mpl socks

calefacción f heating

calidad f quality; **de buena/mala calidad** of good/bad quality

caliente hot; warm

calle f street

calor m heat; **hace calor** it's hot

calzón m (Am) panties, (Br) pants, knickers

calzoncillos mpl underpants (for men)

calzones mpl (Am) panties, (Br) pants, knickers

cama f bed

cámara f camera; **cámara desechable** disposable camera; **cámara digital** digital camera

camarera f waitress

camarero m waiter

cambiar to change; to exchange

cambio m change; exchange; **cambio de sentido** U-turn; **en cambio** on the other hand

caminar to walk

camino m path; way

camión m truck; bus; coach

camisa f shirt

cámping m campsite; **ir de camping** to go camping

campismo m camping

campista mf camper

campo m country, countryside; field, pitch

Canadá m Canada

canadiense Canadian

canadiense mf Canadian

canal m channel; canal

cancelar to cancel

cancha f field, pitch; **cancha de golf** golf course; **cancha de tenis** tennis court

canción f song

canilla f (Am) faucet, (Br) tap

cansado tired

cansador tiring

cantante mf singer

cantar to sing

capilla f chapel

cara f face

caramelo m (Am) candy, (Br) sweet

caravana f (Am) trailer, (Br) caravan, camper; tailback, hold-up

carné m **de conducir** (Am) driver's license, (Br) driving licence

carné m **de identidad** identity card

carnicería f butcher's

caro expensive

carozo m stone, pit (in fruit)

carpa f tent

carretera f road

carrito m (Am) shopping cart, (Br) trolley

carta f letter

cartel m poster

cartera f wallet; (Am) purse, (Br) handbag; briefcase

cartero m (Am) mailman, (Br) postman

casa f house, home; **en casa** at home; **irse a casa** to go home; **casa de campo** villa, cottage; **casa rodante** or **sobre ruedas** (Am) trailer, (Br) caravan, camper

casado married

casco m helmet; **casco antiguo** old town

casi almost, nearly

casilla f **de correos** PO Box

caso m case

castaño brown (hair)

castillo m castle

catedral f cathedral

causa: a causa de because

CD m CD

celular m (Am) cell(phone), (Br) mobile (phone)

cementerio m cemetery

cena f dinner, evening meal

cenar to have dinner

cenicero m ashtray

centímetro m centimetre

centro m centre; **centro comercial** (Am) mall, (Br) shopping centre; **centro de la ciudad** city centre, (Am) downtown

cepillo m brush; **cepillo de dientes** toothbrush

cerca near

cercano near, nearby

cerillo m match

cero zero

cerrado closed, shut

cerrar to close, to shut; **cerrar con llave** to lock

certificado registered

cerveza f beer; **cerveza de barril** draught beer

césped m grass, lawn

chalet m chalet, detached house, villa

champú *m* shampoo
chanclas, chancletas *fpl* flip-flops
chaqueta *f* jacket
chato flat
¡chau! bye!
cheque *m* cheque; cheque de viaje
  traveller's cheque
chica *f* girl
chico little, small
chichón *m* lump, swelling
chimenea *f* chimney
chocante shocking, amazing
chocolate *m* chocolate
chompa *f* sweater, (Br) jumper
chop draught beer
choque *m* shock
cibercafé *m* Internet café
ciclomotor *m* moped
ciclovía *f* (Am) bike path, (Br) cycle path
ciego blind
cielo *m* sky; heaven
cierre *m* (metálico) (Am) zipper, (Br) zip
cigarrillo *m* cigarette
cigarro *m* cigar
cima *f* summit
cine *m* (Am) movie theater, (Br) cinema
cinta *f* Scotch® (Am) Scotch® tape; (Br)
  Sellotape®
cintura *f* waist
cinturón *m* belt; cinturón de seguridad
  safety belt, seat belt
circo *m* circus
cita *f* appointment; hacer *or* marcar *or*
  pedir una cita to make an appointment
ciudad *f* city, town; ciudad vieja old town
Ciudad de México Mexico City
claro light; azul claro light blue; ¡claro!
  of course
clase *f* class; clase turista economy class
clavo *m* nail
clima *m* climate
cobija *f* blanket
cobrar to charge
Coca-cola® Coke®
coche *m* car
cochecito *m* (de bebé) (Am) baby carraige,
  (Br) pram
cocina *f* kitchen; stove; cooking; cocina
  de cámping camping stove; con cocina
  propia self-catering
cocinar cook (v)
código *m* postal (Am) zip code, (Br)
  postcode

coger to catch, to take, to get
cola *f* (Am) line, (Br) queue; hacer cola
  (Am) to wait in line, (Br) to queue
colchón *m* mattress
colección *f* collection
colina *f* hill
color *m* colour
comer to eat; to have lunch
comida *f* food; meal; lunch; comida para
  llevar (Am) takeout, (Br) takeaway;
  comida rápida fast food; hacer la
  comida to do the cooking
comisaría *f* police station
comisión *f* commission
como like
cómo how; ¿cómo? pardon?; ¿cómo
  estás? how are you?
cómodo comfortable
compañía *f* company; compañía aérea
  airline
compartimento *m* compartment
compartir to share
compra *f* shopping; hacer la compra to
  do the shopping
comprar to buy
comprender to understand
compresa *f* (Am) sanitary napkin, (Br)
  sanitary towel
comprobar to check
computadora *f* computer; computadora
  portátil laptop
con with; con gas fizzy
concierto *m* concert
condimento *m* salad dressing
condón *m* condom
conducir to drive
conexión *f* connection
confirmar to confirm
congelador *m* freezer
conocer to know; to meet; la conocí ayer
  I met her yesterday
conseguir to achieve, to manage to do
consejo *m* piece of advice; pedir consejo
  a alguien to ask someone's advice
consigna *f* (Am) baggage room, (Br) left-
  luggage (office)
construir to build
consulado *m* consulate
contactar to contact
contacto *m* contact
contador *m* meter; contador de la luz
  electricity meter
contagioso contagious

contar to count
contestador m **automático** answering machine
contra against
convenir to suit
copa cup *(trophy)*; glass; drink; **tomar una copa** to have a drink; **ir a tomar una copa** to go for a drink
corazón m heart
corbata f tie
correcto right, correct
correo m mail, *(Br)* post; **mandar por correo** to mail, *(Br)* to post; **correo aéreo** airmail; **correo electrónico** e-mail
correos mpl post office
correr to run
cortar to cut; **cortar en rebanadas** to slice; **cortarse** to cut oneself
corto short
cosa f thing
costa f coast
costar to cost; **¿cuánto cuesta?** how much does it cost?
costilla f rib
crecer to grow
creer to believe; to think
crema cream; **crema de afeitar** shaving cream; **crema hidratante** moisturizer; **crema solar** sun cream
cristal m crystal; lens *(of glasses)*
crucero m cruise
crudo raw
cruz f cross
cruzar to cross, to go across
cuaderno m notebook
cuadrado m square
cuadro m painting
¿cuál? which?
cualquier any; **cualquier cosa** anything
cualquiera anybody, anyone
cuándo when
¿cuánto? how much?
¿cuántos? how many?
cuarto m quarter; **un cuarto de hora** a quarter of an hour; **las diez menos cuarto** a quarter to ten
cuarto m room; **cuarto de baño** bathroom
Cuba f Cuba
cubano Cuban
cubano m, **cubana** f Cuban
cubito m **de hielo** ice cube
cubrir to cover
cucaracha f cockroach

cuchara f spoon; **cuchara de servir** tablespoon
cucharita f teaspoon
cuchillo m knife
cuello m neck
cuenco m bowl
cuenta f *(Am)* check, *(Br)* bill
cuerpo m body
¡cuidado! watch out!, careful!
cuidar to look after
cumpleaños mpl birthday
curita f *(Br)* (sticking) plaster, *(Am)* Band-Aid®
cuyo m, **cuya** f whose

D

dañado damaged
dar to give
de of; from; **de... a...** from... to...
debajo de below, under, underneath
deber to owe; must; **¿qué le debo?** how much do I owe you?; **deben de ser las cinco** it must be 5 o'clock; **debo irme** I must go
débil weak
decir to say, to tell; **¿cómo se dice...?** how do you say... ?
declaración f statement
declarar to declare
dedo m finger
dejar to allow, to permit; to leave
delante de in front of
deletrear to spell
delgado thin
demasiado too much; **demasiados** too many; **demasiado** too much; **demasiado hecho** overdone
dentista mf dentist
dentro in; inside; within
departamento m department; apartment
depender to depend; **depende (de)** that depends (on)
dependiente mf sales assistant
deporte m sport
deportivo athletic, sporty
deposito m deposit
derecha f right; **a la derecha (de)** to the right (of)
derecho m right; **tener derecho a ...** to have the right to...
desastre m disaster
desayunar to have breakfast

desayuno *m* breakfast
descansar to rest
descuento *m* discount, concession;
  hacerle a alguien un descuento to give
  someone a discount
desde from, since
desechable disposable
desinfectar to disinfect
desmayarse to faint
desmayo *m* blackout; **sufrir un desmayo**
  to faint
desnudo naked
desodorante *m* deodorant
despacio slowly
despegar to take off
despertador *m* alarm clock
despertar(se) to wake up
después later; **después de** after
detergente *m* detergent, washing powder
detrás: detrás de at the back of, behind
devolución *f* de dinero refund
devolver to return, to give back; **devolver
  el dinero** to refund one's money;
  devolver la llamada to call back
día *m* day
diabetes *f* diabetes
diabético diabetic
diarrea *f* diarrhoea
diciembre *m* December
diente *m* tooth
diesel *m* diesel
dieta *f* diet; **estar a dieta** to be on a diet
diferencia *f* **horaria** time difference
diferente de different (from)
difícil difficult
dinero *m* money; **dinero en efectivo** cash
dirección *f* address; direction
directo direct
dirigir to direct; to manage
discoteca *f* disco, nightclub
disculpa *f* excuse (*n*)
disfrutar to enjoy
disgustado upset
disponible available
divertirse to have fun, to enjoy oneself
doblar to turn
**doce: las doce (del mediodía)/(de la
  noche)** midday, noon/midnight
documentos *mpl* **de identidad** identity
  papers
dólar *m* dollar
doler to hurt; **me duele** it hurts; **me duele
  la cabeza** I have a headache

dolor *m* pain, ache; **dolor de cabeza**
  headache; **tener dolor de garganta** to
  have a sore throat
dolorido painful, sore; sad
domingo *m* Sunday
¿dónde? where?
dormir to sleep
droga *f* drug (*narcotic*)
ducha *f* shower
ducharse to take a shower
dulce sweet
durante during
durar to last
duro hard

E

echar to throw out; **la echo de menos** I
  miss her
edad *f* age
edificio *m* building
él he, el mismo himself (*see grammar*)
el *m* the (*see grammar*)
electricidad *f* electricity
eléctrico electric
ella she (*see grammar*)
ello it (*see grammar*)
ellos *mpl*, **ellas** *fpl* they (*see grammar*)
email *m* e-mail; e-mail address
embajada *f* embassy
embarazada pregnant
embarque *m* boarding
embotellamiento *m* traffic jam
embrague *m* clutch (*of car*)
emergencia *f* emergency
emisora *f* **(de radio)** radio station
empaste *m* filling
empeorar to get worse
empezar to begin, to start
empujar to push
en in; on; **en Inglaterra/2007/español** in
  England/2007/Spanish; **en la mesa** on
  the table
encantado pleased; **¡encantado de
  conocerte!** pleased to meet you!
encantar to love; **me encanta bailar** I
  love dancing
encendedor *m* lighter
encender to light; to turn on, to switch on
enchufar to plug in
enchufe *m* electrical socket
encima de over; above; on
encontrar to find; to meet, to bump into

enero *m* January
enfermedad *f* illness
enfermero *m*, **enfermera** *f* nurse
enfermo sick, ill
enojado angry
enseguida right away
entender to understand
entero whole, complete
entonces then
entrada *f* entrance, way in
entrar to come in; to go in
entre among, between
entreacto *m (Am)* intermission, *(Br)* interval
enviar to send
epiléptico epileptic
equipaje *m* baggage, luggage; **equipaje de mano** hand baggage *or* luggage
equipo *m* equipment; team
equivocado wrong; mistaken; **estás equivocado** you're wrong
error *m* mistake; **cometer un error** to make a mistake
escaleras *fpl* stairs
escape *m* leak
escayola *f* plaster cast
escocer to sting, to burn
escocés Scottish
escocés *m*, **escocesa** *f* Scot
Escocia *f* Scotland
escozor *m* sting, burning sensation
escribir to write; **escribir a máquina** to type; **¿cómo se escribe?** how do you spell it?
escuchar to listen
espalda *f* back
España *f* Spain
español Spanish
español *m*, **española** *f* Spaniard
especia *f* spice
especialidad *f* speciality
espectáculo *m* show
espejo *m* mirror
esperar to wait; to hope; to expect; **¡espere!** hold on!
espiral *f* coil *(contraceptive)*
esponja *f* sponge
esposa *f* wife
esposo *m* husband
espuma *f* **de afeitar** shaving foam
esquí *m* skiing; ski; **esquí acuático** waterskiing
esquiar to ski

esquina corner
estación *f* station; **estación de buses** *or* **camiones** *or* **guaguas** *or* **micros** bus station; **estación de esquí** ski resort; **estación de metro** *or* **subte** *(Am)* subway station, *(Br)* underground station; **estación de tren** train station; **estación de servicio** service station, *(Am)* gas station, *(Br)* petrol station
estacionamiento *m* parking space; *(Am)* parking lot, *(Br)* car park
estacionar to park
estadía *f* stay
estadio *m* stadium
estado *m* state; **Estados Unidos** United States
estadounidense *mf* American
estampilla *f* stamp
estar to be *(see grammar)*
estatura *f* build *(of person)*
este *m* east
este *m*, **esta** *f* this
éste *m*, **ésta** *f* this, this one
estilo *m* style
estómago *m* stomach
éstos *mpl*, **éstas** *fpl* these, these ones
estos *mpl*, **estas** *fpl* these
estreñido constipated
estropeado damaged, ruined
estropear to spoil, to ruin
estudiante *mf* student
estudiar to study
estufa *f* heater; stove
estupendo great
Europa *f* Europe
europeo European
europeo *m*, **europea** *f* European
excepcional exceptional
excepto except
exceso *m* **de equipaje** excess baggage
existencias *fpl* stock
expirado out of date
exposición *f (Am)* exhibit, *(Br)* exhibition
expreso express train
extranjero foreign
extranjero *m*, **extranjera** *f* foreigner; **en el extranjero** abroad
extraño strange

fácil easy
factura *f* bill

facturación f check-in
facturar to check in
falda f skirt
faltar to be missing; **faltan dos...** there are two... missing
familia f family
farmacia f pharmacy, *(Br)* chemist's; **farmacia de guardia** duty pharmacy
faro m lighthouse
favor m favour
favorito favourite
fax m fax
febrero m February
fecha f date; **fecha de caducidad** or **vencimiento** expiry date; **fecha de nacimiento** date of birth
¡felicidades!, ¡felicitaciones! congratulations!
feliz happy
feria f fair *(fi)*
ferry m ferry
festival m festival
fianza f deposit
fiebre f fever; **tener fiebre** to have a temperature
fiesta f party, festival; **fiesta nacional** national holiday; **fiesta oficial** public holiday
fin m end; **fin de semana** weekend
final last, final
final m end; **al final de** at the end of
finalmente finally
fino thin; fine
firmar to sign
flaco thin *(person)*
flash m flash
folleto m brochure, leaflet
fondo m bottom
fontanero m, **fontanera** f plumber
footing m jogging
forma f shape; form; **de todas formas** anyway
formulario m form
fortaleza f fortress
fósforo m match
foto f photo
fractura f fracture
frágil fragile
frasco m flask; bottle
frase f sentence
frazada f blanket
frenar to brake
freno m brake; **freno de mano** handbrake

frente f forehead; **en frente de** opposite
fresco cool
frío cold; **hace frío** it's cold; **tengo frío** I'm cold
frito fried
fuego m fire; **fuegos artificiales** fireworks; **¿tienes fuego?** do you have a light?
fuera outside
fuerte m fort
fuerte strong
fumador m, **fumadora** f smoker
fumar to smoke
funda f **de almohada** pillowcase
fusible m fuse
fútbol m soccer, *(Br)* football; **fútbol americano** *(Am)* football, *(Br)* American football

G

gafas fpl glasses; **gafas de sol** sunglasses
galería f gallery
Gales m Wales
galés Welsh
galés m, **galesa** f Welshman, Welshwoman
garaje m garage
garantía f guarantee; deposit
garganta f throat
garrafa f **de gas** gas cylinder
gas m gas
gasfitero m, **gasfitera** f plumber
gasolina f *(Am)* gas, *(Br)* petrol
gasolinería f *(Am)* gas station, *(Br)* petrol station
gastar to spend
gay mf gay
gel m **de baño** shower gel
gemelos mpl twins; binoculars
general general
genial great
gente f people
gerente mf manager
ginecólogo m, **ginecóloga** f gynaecologist
girar to turn
giro m **postal international** international money order
golf m golf
golpe m blow, knock, bump; shock
gordo fat
gotas drops
gotera f leak
gracias fpl thanks; **gracias a** thanks to; **muchas gracias** thank you very much

grado m degree
gramos mpl grams
Gran Bretaña f Great Britain
grande big
grano m (Am) pimple, (Br) spot
gratis free
grave serious
grifo m (Am) gas station, (Br) petrol station
gringo American; foreign
gringo m, **gringa** f American; foreigner
gripe f flu
gris grey
guagua m bus; coach
guapo good-looking
guardaequipajes m (Am) baggage room, (Br) left-luggage (office)
guía f guidebook; **Guía del ocio** listings magazine; **guía telefónica** directory
guía mf guide
gustar to like; **no me gusta** I don't like it; **me gustaría...** I'd like...

H

habano m cigar
habitación f room
hablar to speak, to talk
hacer to make; to do; **hacer la maleta** to pack
hacia towards; **hacia adelante** forward
hambre: tener hambre to be hungry
hambriento hungry
harto fed up; **estar harto (de)** to be fed up (with)
hasta until, till; **¡hasta luego!** see you later!; **¡hasta pronto!** see you soon!; **¡hasta mañana!** see you tomorrow!
hay there is, there are
hecho m fact; **de hecho** in fact; **hecho a mano** hand-made
heladera f fridge, refrigerator
herida f injury, cut
herido injured, wounded
hermana f sister
hermano m brother
hielo m ice
hierba f herb; grass
hija f daughter
hijo m son
hinchado swollen
hipertensión f high blood pressure
hoja f leaf; sheet of paper; **hoja de afeitar** razor blade

hola! hi!, hello!
hombre m man
hombro m shoulder
homosexual mf homosexual
honesto honest
hora f hour; time; **una hora y media** an hour and a half; **¿qué hora es?** what time is it?; **hora local** local time
horario m timetable
horno m oven
horroroso awful
hospital m hospital
hotel m hotel
hoy today; **hoy en día** nowadays
hueso m stone (in fruit)
huésped mf guest
húmedo damp, wet
humo m smoke (n)
humor m mood; **estar de buen/mal humor** to be in a good/bad mood

I

idioma m language
iglesia f church
igual the same; **me da igual** I don't mind
impermeable (adj) waterproof
impermeable m raincoat
importante important
importar to matter; to mind; **no importa** it doesn't matter; **no me importa** I don't mind
impresión f impression
impuesto m tax
incluido included
incómodo uncomfortable
independiente independent
individual single (room)
infección f infection
inflador m **de bicicleta** bicycle pump
información f information; **información telefónica** (Am) directory assistance, (Br) directory enquiries
Inglaterra f England
inglés English
inglés m, **inglesa** f English
inscribirse to enrol, to sign up
insecticida m insecticide
insecto m insect
insolación f sunstroke; **tener una insolación** to get sunstroke
instrumento m (musical) instrument
intención intention; **tener la intención**

de... to intend to
intentar to try, to attempt
intermitente m (Am) turn signal; (Br) indicator
internacional international
internet f Internet
intoxicación f **alimentaria** food poisoning
inútil useless
invierno m winter
invitar to invite
inyección f injection
ir to go; **ir a buscar** to fetch, to go and get
Irlanda f Ireland
irlandés Irish
irlandés m, **irlandesa** f Irish
irse to leave, to go away
isla f island
isopo m **(de algodón)** (Am) Q-Tip®, (Br) cotton bud
IVA m VAT
izquierda left

J

jabón m soap
jarabe m syrup
jardín m garden
jarra f (Am) pitcher, (Br) jug; **una jarra** a draught beer
jetlag m jetlag
joven young
joven mf young person
joyería f (Am) jewelry store, (Br) jeweller's; jewellery
juego m game
jueves m Thursday
jugar to play
jugo m juice
juguete m toy
julio m July
junio m June
juntos together
justo just; right; fair; **justo en medio** right in the middle; **no es justo** it's not fair

K

kayak m kayak
kilómetro m kilometre

L

la f the (see grammar)

labio m lip
lado m side; **al lado de** at the side of, beside
ladrón m, **ladrona** f thief
lago m lake
lámpara f lamp
lana f wool
lapicera f ballpoint pen
lápiz m pencil; **lápiz de labios** lipstick
largo long
las the; them (see grammar)
lástima f shame, pity; **¡qué lástima!** what a pity!
lata f can, tin
lavabo m washbasin; toilet
lavadora f washing machine
lavandería f (Am) Laundromat®, (Br) launderette
lavar to wash; **lavarse** to wash, to have a wash; **lavarse el pelo** to wash one's hair
lavatorio m washbasin
lavavajillas m dishwasher; washing-up liquid
leer to read
lejos far, a long way
lengua f tongue; language
lentamente slowly
lente f lens; **lentes de contacto** contact lenses; **lentes de sol** sunglasses
lentillas fpl contact lenses
lento slow
levantarse to get up
libra f pound
libre free, available; **libre de impuestos** tax-free
librería f (Am) bookstore, (Br) bookshop; bookshelf
libro m book
limpiar to clean
limpieza f **en seco** dry cleaning
limpio clean
lindo beautiful, lovely (object); good-looking, beautiful (person)
línea f line; **línea de bus** or **camión** or **guagua** or **micro** bus route
linterna f torch
liquidación f sale(s)
lista f list
listo ready
litera f sleeping car, couchette
litro m litre
llamada f call; **llamada a cobro** or **cargo**

revertido, llamada por cobrar *(Am)* collect call, *(Br)* reverse-charge call; **llamada telefónica** phone call

llamar to call, to phone; to call; **llamarse** to be called; **¿cómo te llamas?** what's your name?; **llamar por teléfono** to telephone

llano flat

llave *f* key

llegada *f* arrival

llegar to arrive

llenar to fill

lleno full

llevar to wear; to carry

llorar to cry

llover to rain

lluvia *f* rain

loción *f* lotion; **loción post-solar** aftersun

¡lo siento! sorry!

locutorio *m* cybercafé; public phones

los the; them *(see grammar)*

lucha *f* fight

lugar *m* place

lujo *m* luxury

lujoso luxury

luna *f* moon; **luna de miel** honeymoon

lunes *m* Monday

luz *f* light; lamp; **luz de giro** *(Am)* turn signal; *(Br)* indicator; **luz roja** red light

M

maceta *f* plantpot

madera *f* wood

madre *f* mother

maduro ripe

magnífico great

mal, malo bad

maleta *f* suitcase, case; **hacer la maleta** to pack

maletero *m* *(Am)* trunk, *(Br)* boot *(of car)*

malgastar to waste

malogrado broken, out of order

mancha *f* stain

manejar to drive

manera *f* way, method

manga *f* sleeve

mano *f* hand; **de segunda mano** second-hand

manta *f* blanket

mantener to keep, to maintain

mañana *f* morning; tomorrow; **mañana por la tarde** tomorrow evening;

mañana por la mañana tomorrow morning

mapa *m* map

máquina *f* machine; **máquina de afeitar** electric shaver; **máquina de lavar** washing machine; **máquina de fotos** camera

maquinita *f* **de afeitar** razor

maquinita *f* **eléctrica** (electric) shaver

mar *m* sea

maravilloso wonderful

marcha *f* **atrás** reverse gear

marea *f* tide; **marea alta** high tide; **marea baja** low tide

mareado seasick; dizzy

marido *m* husband

marisco *m* seafood, shellfish

marrón brown

martes *m* Tuesday

marzo *m* March

más more, most; **el más barato** the cheapest one; **más que** more than; **mucho más** much more; **más bien** rather

matar to kill

mayo *m* May

me me; **me miró** she looked at me

mechero *m* lighter

mediano medium, medium-sized

medianoche *f* midnight

medias *fpl* tights

medicamentos *mpl* medicine

medicina *f* medicine

médico *m*, **médica** *f* doctor; **médico general** *or* **de cabecera** GP

medio half, middle; **en medio (de)** in the middle (of); **medio litro/kilo** half a litre/kilo

mediodía *m* midday, noon

mejor better, best; **el mejor** the best; **es mejor...** it's better to...

mejorar to get better, to improve

menos less; least; the least; **al menos** at least

mensaje *m* message

menú *m* menu

menudo: a menudo often

mercado *m* market

mes *m* month

mesa *f* table

mesero *m* waiter

metro *m* metre; **el metro** *(Am)* the subway, *(Br)* the underground

mexicano Mexican
mexicano m, **mexicana** f Mexican
México Mexico (country); Mexico City
mezquita f mosque
mi my
micro m bus; coach
microondas m microwave
miedo: tener miedo (de) to be scared (of)
miembro m member
mientras while
miércoles m Wednesday
minusválido disabled
minuto m minute
mío mine
mirar to look at, to watch
misa f mass
mismo same
mochila f backpack, rucksack
moderno modern
mojado wet
molestar to disturb; **no molestar** do not disturb
momento m moment
monasterio m monastery
moneda f coin; currency
monedero m purse, wallet
montaña f mountain
montañismo m climbing
monumento m monument
morado purple
mordedura f bite
morder to bite
moreno dark-skinned; brown, tanned
morir to die
mosca f fly
mosquito m mosquito
mostrar to show
moto f motorbike
motocicleta f motorcycle, (Br) motorbike
motor m engine
mozo m waiter
mucho a lot; **mucha gente** a lot of people
muelle m quay
muerto dead
mujer f woman; wife
multa f fine
mundo m world
municipalidad f town hall
municipio m town hall
muñeca f wrist
músculo m muscle
museo m museum

música f music
muslo m thigh; leg (of chicken)
muy very; **muy conocido** well-known

N

nada nothing; **de nada** you're welcome
nadar to swim
nadie nobody
nafta f (Am) gas, (Br) petrol
naranja f orange
nariz f nose
natación f swimming
naturaleza f nature
navegación f sailing
navegar to sail, to go sailing
necesario necessary
necesitar to need
negarse to refuse
negro black
nervioso nervous
neumático m tyre
nevar to snow
nevera f fridge, refrigerator
niñera f babysitter
ni... ni... neither ... nor; **ni idea** no idea
nieve f snow
ninguno no; none
niño m, **niña** f child
no no; not (see grammar); **no lo sé** I don't know
no fumador m, **no fumadora** f non-smoker
noche f night; evening; **esta noche** tonight
nombre m name; **nombre de pila** first name; **nombre de soltera** maiden name
normalmente usually
norte m north
norteamericano American
norteamericano m, **norteamericana** f American
nos us (see grammar)
nosotros mpl, **nosotras** fpl we, us (see grammar)
nota f note
noticias fpl news
noviembre m November
novio m, **novia** f boyfriend; fiancé; girlfriend; fiancée
nuestro our
nuestro m, **nuestra** f ours
nuevo new; **de nuevo** again
número m number; size (shoes); **número**

de matrícula registration number;
número de teléfono phone number;
número personal PIN (number)
nunca never

O

o or
objetos *mpl* **perdidos** *(Am)* lost-and-found,
(Br) lost property
obra *f* work; **obra de teatro** play; **obras**
works, roadworks
observar to watch, to observe
obvio obvious
océano *m* ocean
octubre *m* October
ocupado busy; *(Br) (phone)* engaged
ocurrir to happen
odiar to hate
oeste *m* west
oferta *f* offer
ofertas *fpl* sales
oficina *f* office; **oficina de correos** post
office; **oficina de turismo** tourist office
oír to hear
ojo *m* eye
ola *f* wave
oler to smell
olla *f* cooking pot; pan
olor *m* smell
operación *f* operation
operar to operate; **ser operado** to have
an operation
opinión *f* opinion
oportunidad *f* opportunity
óptica *f* optician's
orden order
ordenado tidy
oreja *f* ear
orgánico organic
organizar to organize
orgulloso (de) proud (of)
orquesta *f* orchestra
oscuro dark; **azul oscuro** dark blue
otoño *m* autumn
otro another; other

P

paciente *mf* patient
padre *m* father
padres *mpl* parents
pagar pay

país *m* country
paisaje *m* landscape, scenery
País de Gales *m* Wales
palacio *m* palace
pan *m* bread
panadería *f* baker's
pantalón *m (Am)* pants, *(Br)* trousers;
pantalón corto shorts
pañal *m (Am)* diaper, *(Br)* nappy
paño *m* **de cocina** dish towel
panti *m (Am)* panties, *(Br)* pants, knickers
pañuelo *m* handkerchief; **pañuelo de
papel** tissue
papel *m* paper; **papel higiénico** *or* **de baño**
toilet paper
paquete *m* packet ; package, parcel
par *m* pair
para for; **para que** so that
parabrisas *m (Am)* windshield, *(Br)*
windscreen
parachoques *m* bumper
parada *f* stop; **parada de buses** *or*
camiones *or* **guaguas** *or* **micros** bus stop
paradero *m* **(de buses)** bus stop
paraguas *m* umbrella
parar to stop
parecer to seem, to appear
parecerse a to look like
parking *m (Am)* parking lot, *(Br)* car park
parque *m* park; **parque de atracciones**
funfair; **parque temático** theme park
parrillada *f* barbecue
parte *f* part; **parte delantera** front;
parte superior top; **en todas partes**
everywhere
partido *m* match, game; political party
pasado last; past; **el año pasado** last year;
pasado mañana the day after tomorrow
pasaje *m* ticket; **pasaje de ida** *(Am)* one-
way ticket, *(Br)* single ticket; **pasaje de
ida y vuelta** *(Am)* round-trip ticket, *(Br)*
return ticket
pasajero *m*, **pasajera** *f* passenger
pasaporte *m* passport
pasar to pass; to happen
Pascua *f* Easter
pase *m* pass, permit
paseo *m* walk; **dar un paseo** to go for
a walk
paso *m* step
pasta *f* **de dientes** toothpaste
pastel *m* cake
pastilla *f* tablet

pastor *m*, **pastora** *f* minister *(of the church)*; shepherd, shepherdess

patines *mpl* **en línea** rollerblades

peaje *m* toll

peatón *m*, **peatona** *f* pedestrian

pecho *m* chest

pedazo *m* bit

pedir to order; to ask for; **pedir prestado** to borrow

peine *m* comb

pelar to peel

pelear(se) to argue

película movie, *(Br)* film

peligroso dangerous

pelirrojo red-haired

pelo *m* hair

pelota *f* ball

peluquero *m*, **peluquera** *f* hairdresser

pena *f* shame, pity; **¡que pena!** what a pity!

pendientes *mpl* earrings

pensar to think

pensión *f* boarding-house, guest house; hostel; **pensión completa** *(Am)* American plan, *(Br)* full board; **media pensión** *(Am)* modified American plan, *(Br)* half board

peor worse, worst

pequeño little, small

perder to lose; to miss; **he perdido mis llaves** I've lost my keys; **perdimos el ferry** we missed the ferry

perder to lose

¡perdón! sorry!

perdonar to excuse; **perdona** excuse me

perfecto perfect

perfume *m* perfume

periódico *m* newspaper

periodo *m* period

permitir to allow, to permit, to let

pero but

persona *f* person

Perú *m* Peru

peruano Peruvian

peruano *m*, **peruana** *f* Peruvian

pesado heavy; boring

pescadería *f* fishmonger's, fish shop

pescado *m* fish

picadura *f* sting; bite

picante spicy, hot

picar to bite; to sting; to be spicy

picnic *m* picnic

pie *m* foot

piedra *f* rock, stone

piel *f* skin

pierna *f* leg

pieza *f* piece; **pieza de repuesto** spare part

pila battery

píldora *f* pill; **píldora del día después** morning-after pill

pinchazo *m* puncture

pis: hacer pis to pee

piscina *f* swimming pool

piso *m* storey, floor

placer *m* pleasure

plan *m* plan

plancha *f* iron *(n)*

planchar to iron

planta *f* plant; floor, storey; **planta baja** *(Am)* first floor, *(Br)* ground floor

plástico *m* plastic

plata *f* silver

plataforma *f* platform

plato *m* plate, dish; course; **plato del día** today's special; **plato principal, segundo plato** main course; **lavar los platos** to do the dishes

playa *f* beach; seaside; **en la playa** on the beach, at the seaside

plaza *f* square

plomero *m*, **plomera** *f* plumber

pluma *f* pen

pobre poor

poco little, not much; **poco hecho** rare *(meat)*

pocos few

poder can, be able to; might; **puede ser que llueva** it might rain

policía *f* police; police woman

policía *m* policeman

polvo *m* powder

pomada *f* ointment

poner to put

por for; by; **por ciento** percent; **por favor** please; **¿por qué?** why?; **por separado** separately; **por tanto** so, therefore; **por carretera** by road

posible possible

postal *f* postcard

póster *m* poster

postre *m* dessert

práctico practical

precio *m* price, fare; **precio completo** full price

preferir to prefer

prefijo *m (Am)* dial code, *(Br)* dialling code
pregunta *f* question
preguntar to ask
premio *m* prize
prender to light; to turn on, to switch on
prensa *f* press
preparado ready
preparar to prepare
presión *f* **arterial** blood pressure; **presión alta/baja** high/low blood pressure
prestar to lend
previo previous
primavera *f* spring *(season)*
primero first; **primera clase** first class; **primera planta** *(Am)* second floor, *(Br)* first floor; **en primer lugar** first of all
principal main
principiante *mf* beginner
principio *m* beginning
prisa *f* hurry; **darse prisa** to hurry; **tener prisa** to be in a hurry
prismáticos *mpl* binoculars
privado private
probablemente probably
probador *m* fitting room
probar to try; **probarse** to try on
problema *m* problem; **tener problemas para hacer algo** to have trouble doing something
procesión *f* procession
producto *m* product
profesión *f* profession
profundo deep
programa *m* programme
prohibido forbidden
prometer to promise
prometida *f* fiancée
prometido *m* fiancé
pronóstico *m* forecast; **pronóstico del tiempo** weather forecast
pronto soon
propietario *m*, **propietaria** *f* owner
propina *f* tip
propio own; **mi propio coche** my own car
proponer to propose
propósito *m* purpose
proteger to protect
provecho: ¡buen provecho! enjoy your meal!
público public
pueblo *m* village
puente *m* bridge
puerta *f* door; gate

puerto *m* port, harbour
pulmón *m* lung
punto *m* point; **en punto** o'clock; **las tres en punto** three o'clock; **en su punto** medium *(meat)*; **estar a punto de hacer algo** to be about to do something

Q

que that; which
¿qué? what?; **¿qué quiere?** what do you want?
quedar to arrange to meet; to be left, to remain; **quedarse** to stay
queja *f* complaint
quejarse to complain
quemadura *f* burn
quemar to burn; **quemarse** to get burnt, to burn oneself
querer to want; to love; **querer decir** to mean; **¿qué quiere decir esto?** what does… mean?
querido dear
¿quién? who?; **¿de parte de quién?** who's calling?
quiosco *m* **de revistas** kiosk, newsstand
quitar to remove
quizás maybe, perhaps

R

racista racist
radiador *m* radiator
radio *f* radio
radiografía *f* X-ray
rápidamente quickly
rápido fast, quick
raqueta *f* racket
raramente seldom, rarely
raro rare, uncommon; unusual, strange; **raras veces** seldom, rarely
rascacielos *m* skyscraper
ratón *m* mouse
razonable reasonable
reabrir to reopen
realidad: en realidad in fact
rebaja *f* reduction; **rebajas** sales
rebanada *f* slice
recargo *m* extra charge, supplement
recepción *f* reception
recepcionista *mf* receptionist
receta *f* recipe
recibir to receive

recibo *m* receipt
recogida *f* collection
recomendar to recommend
reconocer to recognize
recordar to remember; to remind
recuerdo *m* souvenir
redondo round
reducido reduced
reducir to reduce
reembolsar to refund
refrigerador(a) *m,f* fridge, refrigerator
refugio *m* **de montaña** mountain hut
regalo *m* present, gift
registro *m* check-in; **hacer el registro** to
    check in
Reino Unido *m* United Kingdom
reírse to laugh
rellenar to fill, to fill in, to fill out
reloj *m* watch
remedios *mpl* medicine
remitente *mf* sender
remontarse a to date (from)
reparar to repair
repetir to repeat
resaca *f* hangover
reservado reserved
reservar to book, to reserve
resfriado *m* cold; **estar resfriado** to have
    a cold
responder to answer
respuesta *f* answer
restaurante *m* restaurant
resto *m* rest
retirar to withdraw
retiro *m* withdrawal
retrasado delayed
retraso *m* delay
retrato *m* portrait
reuma *m* rheumatism
reunión *f* meeting
revelar to develop *(film)*
reventar to burst
revista *f* magazine
riñón *m* kidney
río *m* river
robar to steal
robo *m* theft, robbery; rip-off
rodilla *f* knee
rojo red
rollo *m* film *(for camera)*
romper to break
ropa *f* clothes; **ropa interior** underwear
ropería *f (Am)* coat check; *(Br)* cloakroom

rosa *f* rose
rosado pink
roto broken; out of order
rotonda *f (Am)* traffic circle, *(Br)*
    roundabout
rotura *f* breakdown *(of car)*; **tener una**
    rotura to break down
rueda *f* wheel; **rueda de repuesto** or
    auxiliar spare wheel
ruido *m* noise
ruidoso noisy
ruinas *fpl* ruins
ruta *f* road; **ruta ciclista** *(Am)* bike path,
    (Br) cycle path

S

sábado *m* Saturday
sábana *f* sheet
saber to know, to know how; to taste;
    no sé I don't know; **saber bien** to taste
    good
sabor *m* flavour, taste
sacacorchos *m* corkscrew
saco *m* coat; **saco de dormir** sleeping bag
sal *f* salt
sala *f* hall; room; **sala de conciertos**
    concert hall; **sala de estar** living room
salado salted, salty
salida *f* departure, exit, way out; **salida de**
    emergencia emergency exit
salir to leave, to come out, to go out
salud *f* health; **¡salud!** cheers! *(when*
    drinking); bless you! *(after sneeze)*
salvaje wild
salvar to save, to rescue
sandalias *fpl* sandals
sangrar to bleed
sangre *f* blood
secador *m* **de pelo** hairdrier
secar to dry
seco dry
secundario *m*, **secundaria** *f* high school,
    (Br) secondary school
sed *f* thirst; **tener sed** to be thirsty
segundo second; **segunda clase** second
    class
seguridad *f* safety; security
seguro safe, secure; sure
seguro *m* insurance; **seguro para** or
    contra todo riesgo comprehensive
    insurance
sello *m* stamp

semáforo m traffic light
semana f week; **Semana Santa** Easter, Holy Week
sencillo simple
senderismo m walking, hiking; **hacer senderismo** to go walking
sendero m path
sensación f feeling
sensible sensitive
sentarse to sit down
sentido m sense
sentimiento m feeling
sentir to feel; **sentirse bien/mal** to feel good/bad
señal f sign; signal; **señal de tráfico** road sign
señalero m (Am) turn signal; (Br) indicator
señorita Miss
separar to separate; **separarse** to split up
septiembre m September
ser to be (see grammar)
serio serious
servicio service; **servicio de averías** or **reparaciones** (Am) emergency road service, (Br) breakdown service
servilleta f serviette, napkin
sexo m sex
shock m shock
shot draught beer
si if; **si no** otherwise, if not
sí yes
siempre always
siesta f nap; **echar** or **dormir una siesta** to take a nap
siglo m century
significar to mean; **¿qué significa?** what does it mean?
siguiente next
silencio m silence
silencioso quiet, silent
silla f chair; **silla de ruedas** wheelchair
sillita f (de ruedas) (Am) stroller, (Br) pushchair
silvestre wild
simpático nice, pleasant
sin without
sinagoga f synagogue
sitio m place, spot; **sitio web** website; **en ningún sitio** nowhere; **en todos sitios** everywhere
sobre above; on; **sobre la mesa** on the table
sobre m envelope; **sobre de dormir** sleeping bag

socio m, **socia** f member
¡socorro! help!
sol m sun
sólo only
soltero single, not married
sombra shade
sombrero m hat
sombrilla f beach umbrella
somnífero m sleeping pill
sonreír to smile
sordo deaf
sorprender to surprise
sorpresa f surprise
sostén m bra
sostener to hold
Sr. Mr
Sra. Mrs
su, sus his; her; your; their (see grammar)
submarinismo m scuba diving
subte m (Am) subway, (Br) underground
subtitulado subtitled
sucio dirty
sudar to sweat
suelo m floor; ground
sueño m sleep
suerte f luck
suéter m sweater, (Br) jumper
suficiente enough
sufrir to suffer
sugerir to suggest
supermercado m supermarket
suplemento additional charge, supplement
supuesto: ¡por supuesto! of course!
sur m south
surf: hacer surf to surf, go surfing
surfear to surf, go surfing
surfing m surfing
sutién m bra
suyo, suya, suyos, suyas his; hers; yours; theirs (see grammar)

T

tabaco m tobacco
tabla f plank, board; **tabla de surf** surfboard
tacho m bin; **tacho de la basura** (Am) garbage can, (Br) dustbin
talla f, **talle** f size
tamaño m size
también too, also

tampón *m* tampon

tan so; as

tapa *f* tapa, snack; cover

tapado stuck, jammed; blocked

tapón *m* plug *(bath, sink);* **tapones para los oídos** earplugs

taquilla *f* ticket office

tarde late

tarde *f* afternoon; **por la tarde** in the afternoon

tarjeta *f* card; **tarjeta de crédito** credit card; **tarjeta de débito** debit card; **tarjeta prepago** *(Am)* prepaid card *(for cellphone),* *(Br)* top-up card; **tarjeta telefónica** phonecard

taxi *m* taxi

taxista *mf* taxi driver

taza *f* cup

teatro *m* theatre

tejido *m* material

teléfono *m* phone; **teléfono celular** *(Am)* cellphone, *(Br)* mobile phone

teleobjetivo *m* zoom lens

telesilla *f* chairlift

telesquí *m* ski lift

televisión *f* television

temperatura *f* temperature

templo *m* temple

temporada *f* season

temporal temporary

temprano early

tendero *m*, **tendera** *f (Am)* storekeeper, *(Br)* shopkeeper

tenedor *m* fork

tener to have; **tener que** to have to, must; **tengo que irme** I have to go

tenis *m* tennis

terminal *f* terminal

terminar to finish

termómetro *m* thermometer

terraza *f* terrace

terrible terrible

tía *f* aunt

tibio lukewarm

tiempo *m* weather; time; **hace mal tiempo** the weather's bad

tienda *f (Am)* store, *(Br)* shop; tent; **tienda departamental** or **por departamentos** department store

tierra *f* earth; soil

tijeras *fpl* scissors

tímido shy

tintorería *f* dry cleaner's

tío *m* uncle

típico typical

tipo *m* kind, sort, type; **¿qué tipo de…?** what kind of…?; **tipo de cambio** exchange rate

tipo *m*, **tipa** *f* guy, girl

tirar to throw, to throw away; to pull; **tirarse al agua** to dive

toalla *f* towel; **toalla de baño** bath towel; **toalla higiénica** *(Am)* sanitary napkin, *(Br)* sanitary towel

tobillo *m* ankle

tocar to touch

todavía still; yet

todo, todos all, every; **toda la semana** all week; **todo el tiempo** all the time; **todo incluido** all inclusive; **todo el mundo** everybody, everyone; **todo recto** or **derecho** straight ahead, straight on

tomar to drink; to take, to get; **tomar algo** or **un trago** to have a drink; **tomar el sol** to sunbathe

torcer to turn

torcerse to sprain; **torcerse el tobillo** to sprain one's ankle

tormenta *f* storm

tos *f* cough

toser to cough

trabajar to work

trabajo *m* work; job

tradicional traditional

traducir to translate

traer to bring

tráfico *m* traffic

trago *m* drink; **tomar un trago** to have a drink; **ir a tomar un trago** to go for a drink

traje *m* suit; **traje de baño** swimsuit; **traje isotérmico** wetsuit

tranquilo calm, quiet

transferencia *f* transfer

tranvía *m (Am)* streetcar, *(Br)* tram

través: a través de across; through

tren *m* train

triste sad

trozo *m* piece, bit, slice

tu your*(see grammar)*

tú you *(see grammar)*

turista *mf* tourist

turno *m* turn

tuyo, tuya, tuyos, tuyas yours *(see grammar)*

un *m*, **una** *f* a; one *(see grammar)*
uña nail, fingernail, toenail
urgencia *f* emergency; **la urgencia** *(Am)*
  the emergency room, *(Br)* casualty
urgente urgent; express *(letter)*
usar to use
útil useful

V

vacaciones *fpl (Am)* vacation, *(Br)*
  holiday(s); **de vacaciones** on *(Am)*
  vacation *or (Br)* holiday
vacío empty
vacunado (contra) vaccinated (against)
vagón *m (Am)* car, *(Br)* coach *(on train)*;
  vagón dormitorio *(Am)* sleeping car,
  (Br) couchette
valer to be worth, vale la pena it's worth it
válido valid
valija *f* suitcase; **hacer la valija** to pack
valijero *m (Am)* trunk, *(Br)* boot *(of car)*
valle *m* valley
varios several
vaso *m* glass
vecino *m*, **vecina** *f* neighbour
vegetariano vegetarian
vela *f* candle
velocidad *f* speed
vencido out of date
venda *f*, **vendaje** *m* bandage
vendaje *m* bandage
vendedor *m*, **vendedora** *f* sales assistant
vender to sell
venir to come; **¿te viene bien?** does that
  suit you?
venta *f* sale
ventana *f* window
ventilador *m* electric fan
ver to see
verano *m* summer
verdad: es verdad it's true
verdadero true
verde green
verdulería *f* greengrocer's
vergüenza *f* shame; outrage
Vespa® *f* scooter
vestido *m* dress
vestir to dress; **vestirse** to get dressed
vestuario *m* changing room *(for sports etc)*

vez *f* time; **en vez de** instead of; **de vez
  en cuando** from time to time; **otra vez**
  again; **a veces** sometimes; **una vez**
  once; **dos veces** twice
viajar to travel
viaje *m* trip, journey; **viaje de novios**
  honeymoon; **¡buen viaje!** have a good
  trip!
vida *f* life
vidriera *f* shop window
vidrio *m* glass; lens *(of glasses)*
viento *m* wind
viernes *m* Friday
vino *m* wine; **vino blanco** white wine; **vino
  rosado** rosé wine; **vino tinto** red wine
violar to rape
violeta purple
visa *f* visa
visado *m* visa
visita *f* visit; **visita guiada** guided tour
visitar to visit
vista *f* view; **vista al mar** sea view
vitral *m* stained-glass window
vivir to live
vivo alive
volar to fly
vóleibol *m* volleyball
voltear to turn
volver to return, to come back, to go back
vomitar to vomit
vuelo *m* flight
vuelta *f* return; drive; **dar una vuelta en
  coche** to go for a drive

W

walkman® Walkman®, personal stereo
whisky *m* escocés scotch
windsurf(ing) *m* windsurfing

XYZ

y and; past; **tú y yo** you and I; **las diez y
  cuarto** a quarter past ten
ya already
yeso *f* plaster cast
yo I *(see grammar)*
yo mismo *m*, **yo misma** *f* myself

zapato *m* shoe
zona *f* area
zoo *m*, **zoológico** *m* zoo
zoom *m* zoom lens

GRAMMAR

It is important to **stress** Spanish words correctly; this is easy if you follow these simple rules.

If the word has a written accent, stress the vowel with the accent on it: **fácil**, **ácido**, **préstamo**, televisi**ón**, café.

If the word has no written accent and ends in a vowel, or in -n or -s, stress the second last syllable: bici**cle**ta, tra**ba**jo, **cor**te, **co**men, **me**sas.

If the word has no written accent and ends in any consonant except -n or -s, stress the last syllable: ciu**dad**, fi**nal**, co**mer**, traba**jar**.

Latin American Spanish has three ways of saying *you*: it distinguishes between singular and plural, and between the **polite** and **familiar** forms in the singular. Use the familiar form (tú, *(Arg)* vos) when speaking to friends or children, and the polite form (usted) to strangers, older people or people in authority. The second person singular is tú except in Argentina, where vos is used instead. Note that the present tense verb form for the second person singular is also slightly different in Argentinian Spanish, with the stress being placed on the final syllable:

	Verbs ending in -ar	*Verbs ending in* -er
Standard Spanish	tú hablas	tú sabes
Argentinian Spanish	vos hablás	vos sabés

For verbs ending in -ir, the final syllable becomes -ís in Argentinian Spanish rather than the unstressed -es used in Standard Spanish:

Standard Spanish	tú escribes
Argentinian Spanish	vos escribís

See the verb tables further on for more on conjugations.

In the plural, the polite and familiar forms of address are the same in Latin American Spanish (ustedes), and they use the third person plural verb forms. Note, though, that the pronoun is not necessary, except for emphasis, as the ending of the verb tells you which person is involved. So, there are three ways to ask *how are you?*, for example:

	Singular	Plural
Familiar	¿Cómo estás (tú or (Arg) vos)?	¿Cómo están (ustedes)?
Polite	¿Cómo está (usted)?	¿Cómo están (ustedes)?

Note that there is no separate word for *it* in Spanish: use **él** or **ella** (the words for *he* and *she*) depending on the gender of the word.

To convert a statement into a **question** it is sufficient to use a rising intonation at the end of the sentence; there is no change in word order:

Viene. He's/She's coming. /¿**Viene?** Is he/she coming?
¿**Quién quiere venir?** Who wants to come?

To make a sentence **negative**, simply insert **no** before the verb:

Juan come carne. Juan eats meat.
Juan no come carne. Juan doesn't eat meat.

Spanish nouns are either **masculine** or **feminine**. The **definite article** (*the* in English) and **indefinite article** (*a/an* in English) vary according to whether the noun is masculine or feminine and singular or plural:

	Masc. sing.	Masc. pl.	Fem. sing.	Fem. pl.
Definite	el	los	la	las
Indefinite	un	unos	una	unas

el chico the boy, **los chicos** the boys, **un chico** a boy, **unos chicos** some boys
la chica the girl, **las chicas** the girls, **una chica** a girl, **unas chicas** some girls

The ending of a noun is usually a good indication as to its gender. There are a few exceptions, but most nouns ending in **-o** are masculine and most ending in **-a** are feminine:

el año (year), **el vaso** (glass), **el desayuno** (breakfast)
la semana (week), **la taza** (cup), **la cerveza** (beer)

Some common exceptions are: el día (day), el problema (problem), el idioma (language), el clima (climate), la mano (hand), la radio (radio), la foto (photo), la moto (motorbike).

As for other endings, nouns ending in -or are masculine: el congelador (freezer), el amor (love); and those in -ción, -sión, -tad and -dad are feminine: la estación (station), la ciudad (town, city).

The **plural** of nouns is formed by adding -s if the singular ends in a vowel, and -es if it ends in a consonant:

> mesa → mesas (tables), cuchillo → cuchillos (knives)
> hotel → hoteles (hotels), tren → trenes (trains)

Note that a final -z changes to -ces in the plural.

> una vez (once), dos veces (twice); un pez (a fish), dos peces (two fishes)

Adjectives in Spanish agree with nouns in number and gender and usually go after the noun:

> un vino blanco (a white wine), dos vinos blancos (two white wines)
> una calle estrecha (a narrow street), calles estrechas (narrow streets)

In the mini-dictionary in this phrasebook, we give the masculine singular and feminine singular forms of adjectives. The plural of adjectives is formed in the same way as for nouns:

> bonito, bonita, bonitos, bonitas (beautiful)
> caro, cara, caros, caras (dear, expensive)

Note how the feminine and plural of some other adjectives are formed:

> inglés, inglesa, ingleses, inglesas (English)
> catalán, catalana, catalanes, catalanas (Catalan)
> encantador, encantadora, encantadores, encantadoras (charming)

Possessive adjectives (*my*, *your*, *his* etc) in Spanish are as follows:

Singular	**mi, mis** (my)
	tu, tus (your1)
	su, sus (his, her, its, your2)
Plural	**nuestro, nuestra, nuestros, nuestras** (our)
	su, sus (your1&2)
	su, sus (their)

1 Familiar form of address. 2 Polite form of address.

Note that Spanish does not distinguish between *his*, *her* and *its*: **su/sus** is used for all of them. **Su/sus** is also used to translate *your* when using the polite or plural form of address. While all possessive adjectives have a plural form, only **nuestro/a** has separate feminine forms.

mi hermano (my brother), **mis hermanas** (my sisters)
tu libro (your book), **tus bolsas** (your bags)
nuestro coche (our car), **nuestras novias** (our girlfriends)
su hijo (his/her/their/your son), **sus hijas** (his/her/their/your daughters)

Most **adverbs** are formed by taking the feminine singular form of the adjective and adding **-mente**:

perfecto → perfectamente (perfectly)

Two common adverbs not formed like this are **bien** (*well*) and **mal** (*badly*).

Subject pronouns (*I*, *we* etc) are generally not required in Spanish, except for emphasis as the verb ending indicates who the subject is. It is enough to say, for example: **voy** (I go), **vamos** (we go), **van** (they go), etc.

yo (I)	nosotros/nosotras (us)
tú, *(Arg)* vos (you1)	ustedes (you1&2)
él (him), ella (her), usted (you2)	ellos/ellas (them)

1 Familiar form of address. 2 Polite form of address.

Remember that the 2nd person plural (**ustedes**) is used for both familiar and polite forms, and shares its verb form with the 3rd person plural (**ellos/ellas**).

Spanish pronouns may seem more complex than in English; for example, you must distinguish between direct object and indirect object pronouns in the third person:

Direct object	**Lo** vi ayer. I saw **him** yesterday.	
	La vi hace una semana. I saw **her** a week ago.	
Indirect object	**Le** di un regalo. I gave **him/her** a present.	
	Le pedí un cigarro. I asked him/her for a cigarette.	

Note that you must insert the preposition **a** before the direct object when the direct object is a person:

Conocen a Pedro. They know Pedro.

Remember also that a different form is used after a preposition in the 1st and 2nd person singular:

Te he traído un regalo. I have brought you a present.
Tengo un regalo para **ti**. I have a present for you.

For reference, here is the table of subject, object and reflexive pronouns:

	Subject	Direct object	Indirect object	After preposition	Reflexive
Singular	yo	me	me	mí	me
	tú, (Arg)	te	te	ti, (Arg)	te
	vos			vos	
	él	lo	le	él	se
	ella	la	le	ella	se
	usted	lo/la	le	usted	se
Plural	nosotros/ nosotras	nos	nos	nosotros/ nostras	nos
	ustedes	los/las	les	ustedes	se
	ellos	los	les	ellos	se
	ellas	las	les	ellas	se

Possessive pronouns are words like *mine*, *hers* and *ours*, for example:

Este asiento es **el mío**, **el tuyo** es ése. This seat is **mine**, **yours** is that one.

Here is the list for reference:

(el) mío, (la) mía, (los) míos, (las) mías (mine)
(el) tuyo, (la) tuya, (los) tuyos, (las) tuyas (yours1)
(el) suyo, (la) suya, (los) suyos, (las) suyas (his, hers, yours2)
(el) nuestro, (la) nuestra, (los) nuestros, (las) nuestras (ours)
(el) suyo, (la) suya, (los) suyos, (las) suyas (yours1&2)
(el) suyo, (la) suya, (los) suyos, (las) suyas (theirs)

1 Familiar form of address. 2 Polite form of address

Remember that the 2nd person plural (**ustedes**) is used for both familiar and polite forms, and shares its verb form with the 3rd person plural (**ellos/ellas**).

Reflexive verbs are used when the subject and the object of a verb are the same person and they are constructed with **reflexive pronouns** (see table page 179 – in English *myself*, *yourself* etc). These reflexive pronouns are not always free-standing; they are tagged onto infinitives, imperatives and gerunds, so in the mini-dictionary reflexive verbs all end in -se, eg acordarse (to remember).

Me compró un vestido nuevo. I bought **myself** a new dress.
Se sentó y empezó a comer. He sat **himself** down and started to eat.

However, they are much more common in Spanish, and do not always translate into English with a -*self* pronoun because English often expresses the idea differently:

Me levanto, **me** ducho y **me** visto. I get up, I have a shower and I get dressed.

¡Lávate, aféitate y vístete! Have a wash, have a shave and get dressed!

Reflexive verbs are also used when there is a mutual action involved:

Nos conocimos en una fiesta. We met (each other) at a party.

But in other cases it might not be so clear why a Spanish verb is reflexive:

Se fueron sin decir adiós. They left without saying goodbye.
No **me** acuerdo de su nombre. I don't remember her name.

Spanish **verbs** are divided into three groups (conjugations), ending in -ar,
-er and -ir.

Here is the present tense of three regular verbs, one from each conjugation.
A hyphen has been inserted only so that you can see the endings more clearly.
Notice how the Argentinian **vos** form (familiar second person singular) differs
slightly from the **tú** equivalent used in other countries.

	hablar	**comer**	**vivir**
	(to speak)	*(to eat)*	*(to live)*
yo	habl-**o**	com-**o**	viv-**o**
tú, *(Arg)* vos	habl-**as**,	com-**es**,	viv-**es**,
	(Arg) habl-**ás**	*(Arg)* com-**és**	*(Arg)* viv-**ís**
él/ella/usted	habl-**a**	com-**e**	viv-**e**
nosotros/	habl-**amos**	com-**emos**	viv-**imos**
nosotras			
ustedes	habl-**an**	com-**en**	viv-**en**
ellos/ellas	habl-**an**	com-**en**	viv-**en**

Remember that the 2nd person plural (**ustedes**) is used for both familiar and
polite forms, and shares its verb form with the 3rd person plural (**ellos/ellas**).

Habla muy bien español. He/She speaks/You speak very good Spanish.
No como carne. I don't eat meat.
¿Dónde vives *or (Arg)* vivís? Where do you live?

Irregular verbs undergo certain spelling changes, which you will have to
learn.

Here are some common irregular verbs in the present tense :

	tener *(to have)*	**ir** *(to go)*	**querer** *(to want)*
yo	tengo	voy	quiero
tú, *(Arg)* vos	tienes, *(Arg)* tenés	vas	quieres, *(Arg)* querés
él/ella/usted	tiene	va	quiere
nosotros/ nosotras	tenemos	vamos	queremos
ustedes	tienen	van	quieren
ellos/ellas	tienen	van	quieren

	venir *(to come)*	**haber** *(to have)*	**poder** *(to be able to, can)*
yo	vengo	he	puedo
tú, *(Arg)* vos	vienes, *(Arg)* venís	has	puedes, *(Arg)* podés
él/ella/usted	viene	ha	puede
nosotros/ nosotras	venimos	hemos	podemos
ustedes	vienen	han	pueden
ellos/ellas	vienen	han	pueden

Remember that the 2nd person plural (**ustedes**) is used for both familiar and polite forms, and shares its verb form with the 3rd person plural (**ellos/ellas**).

Note that **haber** is also an auxiliary verb and can be used to form the present perfect tense:

He comprado un libro. I've bought a book.
¿Has visto esta película? Have you seen this film?
No hemos comido nada. We haven't eaten anything.

Some verbs are irregular only in the 1st person singular:

hacer (to do, make): hago, haces or *(Arg)* hacés, hace...
saber (to know - something): sé, sabes or *(Arg)* sabés, sabe...
conocer (to know - someone): conozco, conoces or *(Arg)* conocés, conoce...

Note there are two Spanish verbs which translate the English *to be*, **ser** and **estar**. The basic difference between the two is that **ser** describes permanent states and inherent qualities, whereas **estar** describes temporary situations and geographical location. Here is the present tense of both:

ser: soy, eres *or (Arg)* sos, es, somos, son, son
estar: estoy, estás, está, estamos, están, están

Es inglés. He's English.
Su mujer **es** alta. His wife is tall.
Están de vacaciones. They're on holiday.
El hotel **está** cerca de la playa. The hotel is near the beach.

The **imperfect** of regular verbs is as follows. This tense is used to denote a continuous action in the past (eg I **was talking** to him). Note that -er and -ir verbs have the same endings:

	hablar	**comer**	**vivir**
yo	habl-**aba**	com-**ía**	viv-**ía**
tú, *(Arg)* vos	habl-**abas**	com-**ías**	viv-**ías**
él/ella/usted	habl-**aba**	com-**ía**	viv-**ía**
nosotros/ nosotras	habl-**ábamos**	com-**íamos**	viv-**íamos**
ustedes	habl-**aban**	com-**ían**	viv-**ían**
ellos/ellas	habl-**aban**	com-**ían**	viv-**ían**

Remember that the 2nd person plural (**ustedes**) is used for both familiar and polite forms, and shares its verb form with the 3rd person plural (**ellos/ellas**).

The verb **estar** is regular in the imperfect; **ser** is conjugated as follows:

era, eras, era, éramos, eran, eran

The **simple past** of regular verbs is as follows. This tense is used to denote a single action, or an action seen as shortlived, in the past (eg I **saw** him yesterday). Note that -er and -ir verbs have the same endings:

GRAMMAR

	hablar	**comer**	**vivir**
yo	habl-**é**	com-**í**	viv-**í**
tú, *(Arg)* vos	habl-**aste**	com-**iste**	viv-**iste**
él/ella/usted	habl-**ó**	com-**ió**	viv-**ió**
nosotros/ nosotras	habl-**amos**	com-**imos**	viv-**imos**
ustedes	habl-**aron**	com-**ieron**	viv-**ieron**
ellos/ellas	habl-**aron**	com-**ieron**	viv-**ieron**

Remember that the 2nd person plural (**ustedes**) is used for both familiar and polite forms, and shares its verb form with the 3rd person plural (**ellos/ellas**).

Notice how these two tenses are used:

Llovía fuerte, así que **llevé** el paraguas. It **was raining** hard, so I **took** my umbrella.
Caminaba por el bosque cuando **empezó** a llover. I **was walking** through the forest when it **started** to rain.
Antes **vivía** en el campo. I **used to live** in the country.
Viví tres meses en Madrid. I **lived** in Madrid for three months.

The past simple of **ser** and **estar** is as follows:

fui, fuiste, fue, fuimos, fueron, fueron
estuve, estuviste, estuvo, estuvimos, estuvieron, estuvieron

To form the future tense, simply add the following endings onto the infinitive: -é, -ás, -á, -emos, -án, -án.

hablar: hablaré, hablarás, hablará, hablaremos, hablarán, hablarán

Hablaré con él mañana. I'll talk to him tomorrow.
El tren llegará en seguida. The train will arrive shortly.

HOLIDAYS AND FESTIVALS

NATIONAL BANK HOLIDAYS

In Latin America, bank holidays are known as **días feriados**. Administrative departments, banks, offices and most shops are closed, but most bars, restaurants, museums and other tourist attractions remain open (albeit with restricted opening hours).

1 January	**día de Año Nuevo** (New Year's Day), *(Cuba)* **Aniversario de la Revolución** (Revolution Day)
6 January	**Día de los Reyes Magos** (Epiphany)
February	**Carnaval** (Carnival)
5 February	*(Mex)* **Día de la Constitución** (Constitution Day)
March/April	**Semana Santa** (Holy week)
March/April	**Viernes Santo** (Good Friday)
21 March	*(Mex)* **Natalicio de Benito Juárez** (Birth of Benito Juárez)
1 May	**Día del Trabajo** (Labour Day)
25 May	*(Arg)* **Día nacional** (National Day)
29 June	*(Peru)* **San Pedro y San Pablo** (Saint Pedro and Saint Pablo's Day)
9 July	*(Arg)* **Día de la Independencia** (Independence Day)
25-27 July	*(Cuba)* **Aniversario del asalto al Cuartel Moncada** (National week)
28-29 July	*(Peru)* **Fiestas Patrias** (Independence Day)
30 August	*(Peru)* **Santa Rosa de Lima** (Saint Rose of Lima's Day)
14-16 September	*(Mex)* **Fiestas Patrias** (Independence Day)
8 October	*(Peru)* **Combate de Angamos** (Battle of Angamos)
10 October	*(Cuba)* **Guerras de la Independencia** (Independence war)
12 October	**Día de la Raza** (Columbus Day)

1-2 November	**Día de todos los Santos** (All Saints' Day)
8 December	*(Peru)* **Inmaculada Concepción** (Immaculate Conception)
12 December	*(Mex)* **Virgen de Guadalupe**
25 December	**Navidad** (Christmas Day)

FESTIVALS

There always seems to be a festival going on somewhere in Latin America. Many traditional religious festivals are still observed, but all the celebrations are an opportunity to have a good time. In the summer, every village has its own festival in Peru. Here are just a few of the best-known and most impressive:

February

The **Fiesta de La Candelaria** is celebrated at Xochimilco, Mexico. In Puno, Peru, there are celebrations throughout the month but particularly on the 2nd, when there are dances and religious services.

Carnivals are held all over Peru: the **carnaval de Cajamarca** is without a doubt the most famous. Groups of people in fancy dress known as **patrullas** parade through the streets, portraying the year's major social, cultural and political events through satirical songs (**coplas**), which are specially written for the occasion. In Argentina, the Carnival celebrations in the North, particularly at Humahuaca, are very popular with locals.

March-April

In Mexico, **Corpus Christi** Thursday is widely celebrated at cathedrals. **Semana Santa** (Holy Week or Easter Week) is the largest and most important national holiday besides Christmas. The most impressive celebrations take place in Xochimilco and Iztapalapa.

June	St. John´s day in Mexico, with particular celebrations in Coyoacán. In Cusco, the annual **Inti Raimy** (Festival of the Sun) takes place on the 24th in the Sacsahuaman fortress, and the **Qoyllur Riti** (Snow Star) is in early June. Groups of **ukukus** (men dressed as bears) go to the top of Mount Ausangate to collect huge blocks of ice. They return three days later, to be welcomed by crowds of people dancing, drinking and praying at the bottom of the mountain.
July	The **Día de la Virgen del Carmen** is celebrated in Mexico with a flower market at San Ángel. In Peru, Independence Day is celebrated on July 28th, but the 29th is also a holiday. Parades and civic ceremonies are held all over the country.
September	Independence week is celebrated in Mexico from the 13th to the 16th.
October	Month of the **Señor de los Milagros** (Lord of the Miracles). Festivities are held in Lima.
November	The celebrations for **Día de los muertos** on the 1st and 2nd are very special in Mexico: people eat, drink, sing and visit cemeteries where loved ones are buried.
December	In Mexico, the festival of the **Virgen de Guadalupe** honours Mexico's patron saint. There are religious processions and street festivals full of food, drink, music and dancing.

USEFUL ADDRESSES

ARGENTINA
American Embassy in Buenos Aires
Avenida Colombia 4300
Buenos Aires
Tel: +54 (11) 5777 4533 / Fax: +54 (11) 5777 4240
http://buenosaires.usembassy.gov

Canadian Embassy in Buenos Aires (also for Paraguay)
Street address: Calle Tagle 2828
Buenos Aires
Mailing address: Casilla de Correo 1598
Buenos Aires
Tel: (54-11) 4808-1000 / Fax: 54-11-4808-1111
www.dfait-maeci.gc.ca/latin-america/argentina/

British Embassy in Buenos Aires
Calle Luis Agote 2412
1425 Buenos Aires
Tel: +54 (11) 4808 2200 / Fax: +54 (11) 4808 2274
www.britain.org.ar

CUBA
British Embassy in Havana
Calle 34 No. 702-4 entre 7ma Avenida y 17
Miramar
La Habana
Tel: +53 (7) 204 1771 / Fax: +53 (7) 204 8104
www.britishembassy.gov.uk/cuba

MEXICO
American Embassy in Mexico City
Paseo de la Reforma 305
Colonia Cuauhtémoc
06500 México D.F.
Tel: +52 (55) 5080 2000 / Fax: +52 (55) 5511 9980
http://mexico.usembassy.gov/

Canadian Embassy in Mexico City
Schiller 529
Colonia Polanco
11560 México D.F.
Tel: +52 (55) 5724 7900 / Fax: +52 (55) 5724 7980
www.dfait-maeci.gc.ca/mexico-city/

British Embassy in Mexico City
Río Lerma 71
Colonia Cuauhtémoc
06500 México D.F.
Tel: +52 (55) 5242 8500 / Fax: +52 (55) 5242 8517
www.britishembassy.gov.uk/mexico

PERU
American Embassy in Lima
Avenida La Encalada cdra. 17 s/n
Surco
Lima 33
Tel: +51 (1) 434 3000 / Fax: +51 (1) 618 2397
http://lima.usembassy.gov

Canadian Embassy in Lima
Street address: Libertad 130
Miraflores
Lima 18
Mailing address: Casilla 18-1126
Correo Miraflores
Lima
Tel: +51 (1) 444 4015 / Fax: +51 (1) 242 4050
www.dfait-maeci.gc.ca/latin-america/peru

British Embassy in Lima
Torre Parque Mar, piso 23
Avenida José Larco 1301
Miraflores
Lima 18
Tel: +51 (1) 617 3050 / Fax: +51 (1) 617 3055
www.britishembassy.gov.uk/peru

DOMINICAN REPUBLIC
American Embassy in Santo Domingo
Colle Cesar Nicolas Penson
Colle Leopoldo Navarro, Unidad 5500
Santo Domingo
Tel: +1 (809) 541 2171 / Fax: +1 (809) 686 7437
http://santodomingo.usembassy.gov/

Canadian Embassy in Santo Domingo
Street address: Capitán Eugenio de Marchena No. 39
La Esperilla
Santo Domingo
Mailing address: A.P. 2054
Santo Domingo
Tel: +1 (809) 685 1136 / +1 200 0012 / Fax: +1 (809) 682 2691
www.dfait-maeci.gc.ca/latin-america/dominicanrepublic

British Embassy in Santo Domingo
Avenida 27 de Febrero No 233
Edificio Corominas Pepin
Santo Domingo
Tel: +1 (809) 472 7905 / Fax: +1 (809) 472 7190
www.britishembassy.gov.uk/dominicanrepublic

CONVERSION TABLES

Note that when writing numbers, Spanish uses a comma where English uses a full stop. For example, 0.6 would be written 0,6 in Spanish.

Measurements

Only the metric system is used in Latin America.

Length
1 cm ≈ 0.4 inches
30 cm ≈ 1 foot

Distance
1 metre ≈ 1 yard
1 km ≈ 0.6 miles

To convert kilometers into miles, divide by 8 and then multiply by 5.
To convert miles into kilometers, divide by 5 and then multiply by 8.

kilometers	1	2	5	10	20	100
miles	0.6	1.25	3.1	6.25	12.50	62.5

Weight
25g ≈ 1 oz   1 kg ≈ 2 lb   6 kg ≈ 1 stone

To convert kilos into pounds, divide by 5 and then multiply by 11.
To convert pounds into kilos, multiply by 5 and then divide by 11.

kilos	1	2	10	20	60	80
pounds	2.2	4.4	22	44	132	176

Liquid
1 litre ≈ 2 pints   4.5 litres ≈ 1 gallon

Temperature
To convert temperatures in Celsius into Fahrenheit, divide by 5, multiply by 9 and then add 32. To convert temperatures in Fahrenheit into Celsius, subtract 32, multiply by 5 and then divide by 9.

Celsius (°C)	0	4	10	15	20	25	30	38
Fahrenheit (°F)	32	40	50	59	68	77	86	100

Clothes sizes

Sometimes you will find sizes given using the English-language abbreviations **XS** (Extra Small), **S** (Small), **M** (Medium), **L** (Large) and **XL** (Extra Large), or the Spanish-language ones **PP** (muy pequeño), **P** (pequeño), **M** (mediano), **G** (grande), **GG** (súper grande).

• Women's clothes

Latin America	34	36	38	40	42	44	etc
USA	4	6	8	10	12	14	
UK	6	8	10	12	14	16	

• Bras

Latin America	70	75	80	85	90	etc
USA/UK	32	34	36	38	40	
Latin America/UK	A	B	C	D	DD	etc
USA	AA	A	B	C	D	

• Men's shirts (collar size)

Latin America	36	38	41	43	etc
USA/UK	14	15	16	17	

• Men's clothes

Latin America	40	42	44	46	48	50	etc
USA/UK	30	32	34	36	38	40	

• Women's shoes

Latin America	37	38	39	40	42	etc
USA	6.5	7.5	8.5	9.5	10.5	
UK	4	5	6	7	8	

• Men's shoes

Latin America	40	42	43	44	46	etc
USA	7.5	8.5	9.5	10.5	11.5	
UK	7	8	9	10	11	